my revisi⏻n notes

'er

AQA AS
LAW

Peter Darwent
Ian Yule

HODDER
EDUCATION

Although every effort has been made to ensure that website addresses are correct at time of going to press, Hodder Education cannot be held responsible for the content of any website mentioned in this book. It is sometimes possible to find a relocated web page by typing in the address of the home page for a website in the URL window of your browser.

Hachette UK's policy is to use papers that are natural, renewable and recyclable products and made from wood grown in sustainable forests. The logging and manufacturing processes are expected to conform to the environmental regulations of the country of origin.

Orders: please contact Bookpoint Ltd, 130 Milton Park, Abingdon, Oxon OX14 4SB. Telephone: +44 (0)1235 827720. Fax: +44 (0)1235 400454. Lines are open 9.00a.m.–5.00p.m., Monday to Saturday, with a 24-hour message answering service. Visit our website at www.hoddereducation.co.uk

First published in 2014 by
Hodder Education,
An Hachette UK Company
338 Euston Road
London NW1 3BH
Impression number   10 9 8 7 6 5 4 3 2
Year   2018 2017 2016 2015

Cover photo © iStock/Thinkstock
Artwork by Datapage (India) Pvt. Ltd.
Typeset in Cronos Pro-Light 12/14 by Datapage (India) Pvt. Ltd.
Printed in India
A catalogue record for this title is available from the British Library
ISBN 978 14718 07152

Get the most from this book

Everyone has to decide his or her own revision strategy, but it is essential to review your work, learn it and test your understanding. These Revision Notes will help you to do that in a planned way, topic by topic. Use this book as the cornerstone of your revision and don't hesitate to write in it — personalise your notes and check your progress by ticking off each section as you revise.

☑ Tick to track your progress

Use the revision planner on pages 4 and 5 to plan your revision, topic by topic. Tick each box when you have:

● revised and understood a topic

● tested yourself

● practised the exam questions and gone online to check your answers and complete the quick quizzes

You can also keep track of your revision by ticking off each topic heading in the book. You may find it helpful to add your own notes as you work through each topic.

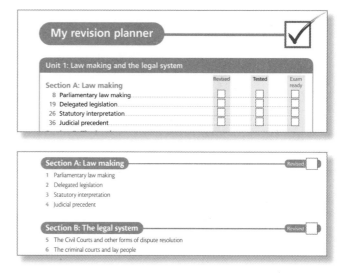

Features to help you succeed

Exam tips and summaries

Throughout the book there are tips to help you boost your final grade.

Summaries provide advice on how to approach each topic in the exams, and suggest other things you might want to mention to gain those valuable extra marks.

Typical mistakes

Examples of the typical mistakes candidates make and how you can avoid them.

Key terms

Clear, concise definitions of essential key terms are provided on the page where they appear.

Key words from the specification are highlighted in bold for you throughout the book.

Exam practice

Practice exam questions are provided for each topic. Use them to consolidate your revision and practise your exam skills.

Now test yourself

These short, knowledge-based questions provide the first step in testing your learning. Answers are at the back of the book.

Online

Go online to check your answers to the exam questions at **www.therevisionbutton.co.uk/ myrevisionnotes**

Check your understanding

Use the questions that have been set at the end of the topic to make sure that you understand each topic. Answers are at the back of the book.

My revision planner

Unit 1: Law making and the legal system

		Revised	Tested	Exam ready
Section A: Law making				
8	Parliamentary law making	☐	☐	☐
19	Delegated legislation	☐	☐	☐
25	Statutory interpretation	☐	☐	☐
35	Judicial precedent	☐	☐	☐
Section B: The legal system				
42	The Civil Courts and other forms of dispute resolution	☐	☐	☐
53	The criminal courts and lay people	☐	☐	☐
63	The legal profession and other sources of advice and funding	☐	☐	☐
74	The judiciary	☐	☐	☐

Unit 2: The concept of liability

		Revised	Tested	Exam ready
Section A: Introduction to criminal liability				
84	Underlying principles of criminal liability including non-fatal offences	☐	☐	☐
94	The courts: procedure and sentencing	☐	☐	☐
Section B: Introduction to tort				
100	Liability in negligence	☐	☐	☐
106	The courts: procedure and damages	☐	☐	☐
Section C: Introduction to contract				
111	Formation of contract	☐	☐	☐
120	Breach of contract and the courts: procedure and damages	☐	☐	☐

126 Now test yourself and Check your understanding answers
Exam practice answers and quick quizzes at www.therevisionbutton.co.uk/myrevisionnotes

Countdown to my exams

6–8 weeks to go

- Start by looking at the specification — make sure you know exactly what material you need to revise and the style of the examination. Use the revision planner on page 4 to familiarise yourself with the topics.
- Organise your notes, making sure you have covered everything on the specification. The revision planner will help you to group your notes into topics.
- Work out a realistic revision plan that will allow you time for relaxation. Set aside days and times for all the subjects that you need to study, and stick to your timetable.
- Set yourself sensible targets. Break your revision down into focused sessions of around 40 minutes, divided by breaks. These Revision Notes organise the basic facts into short, memorable sections to make revising easier.

Revised ☐

4–6 weeks to go

- Read through the relevant sections of this book and refer to the examiner's tips, examiner's summaries, typical mistakes and key terms. Tick off the topics as you feel confident about them. Highlight those topics you find difficult and look at them again in detail.
- Test your understanding of each topic by working through the 'Now test yourself' questions in the book. Look up the answers at the back of the book.
- Make a note of any problem areas as you revise, and ask your teacher to go over these in class.
- Look at past papers. They are one of the best ways to revise and practise your exam skills. Write or prepare planned answers to the exam practice questions provided in this book. Check your answers online and try out the extra quick quizzes at **www.therevisionbutton.co.uk/ myrevisionnotes**
- Use the revision activities to try different revision methods. For example, you can make notes using mind maps, spider diagrams or flash cards.
- Track your progress using the revision planner and give yourself a reward when you have achieved your target.

Revised ☐

One week to go

- Try to fit in at least one more timed practice of an entire past paper and seek feedback from your teacher, comparing your work closely with the mark scheme.
- Check the revision planner to make sure you haven't missed out any topics. Brush up on any areas of difficulty by talking them over with a friend or getting help from your teacher.
- Attend any revision classes put on by your teacher. Remember, he or she is an expert at preparing people for examinations.

Revised ☐

The day before the examination

- Flick through these Revision Notes for useful reminders, for example the exam tips, summaries, typical mistakes and key terms.
- Check the time and place of your examination.
- Make sure you have everything you need — extra pens and pencils, tissues, a watch, bottled water, sweets.
- Allow some time to relax and have an early night to ensure you are fresh and alert for the examinations.

Revised ☐

My exams

AS LAW01

Date: . . . .

Time: . . . .

Location: . . . .

AS LAW02

Date: . . . .

Time: . . . .

Location: . . . .

Introduction to Unit 1: Law making and the legal system

Unit 1 is divided into the following:

Section A: Law making

1 Parliamentary law making
2 Delegated legislation
3 Statutory interpretation
4 Judicial precedent

Section B: The legal system

5 The Civil Courts and other forms of dispute resolution
6 The criminal courts and lay people
7 The legal profession and other sources of advice, and funding
8 The judiciary

The Unit 1 exam

- The exam lasts 1 hour 30 minutes and you are required to answer questions on three topics – one topic from Section A, one topic from Section B and one topic from Section A *or* Section B.
- The exam will include questions on all the topics in Unit 1. Each topic has three exam questions, each worth 10 marks.
- The first two exam questions test understanding of legal rules and principles (AO1). These questions will involve describing, explaining or outlining.
- The third exam question tests analysis and evaluation (AO2) and carries an additional 2 marks for quality of written communication (AO3). This question usually involves discussing advantages or disadvantages.

Help from the exam board

- The AQA specification provides lots of important information and guidance. It tells you what you need to cover in each topic, explains the assessment objectives (AOs) and gives performance descriptions showing the skills typically required to achieve a Grade A and a Grade E.
- The AQA website also has past papers, mark schemes and examiner reports.

Exam practice answers and quick quizzes at **www.therevisionbutton.co.uk/myrevisionnotes**

Preparing for the exam

- It is important to look at the material provided by the exam board, especially past papers, so that you can see what kind of questions are asked on each topic.

- You must be prepared to answer all the potential questions that may be asked on the topics you have chosen. The material in this guide will help you do this, but you should also look at questions that have been set in past papers and at the mark schemes and examiner reports in order to be confident that you are properly prepared.

- To achieve high marks answers need to provide information which is relevant to the question being asked. The level of detail needed will depend on the question. For example, a two-part question will expect less detail on each part than a whole question on just one aspect.

- Answers which are thin and generalised will not achieve high marks. Learn the material thoroughly, so that you go into the exam with the appropriate knowledge.

- You also need to understand what you are learning, so that you can adapt it to answer questions that are slightly different to those that you may have answered before.

- In a question on advantages and disadvantages you should aim to discuss at least three. Also note that examiners are looking for more than a list. They want you to develop your answer and comment on why that point is an advantage or disadvantage.

- In the exam you will have to write nine separate answers in 90 minutes. Practice in answering questions under exam conditions is very important. You must be confident that you can write each answer in 10 minutes and cover everything required by the question.

Use of authorities

- In many Unit 1 answers you will need to refer to authorities – cases or Acts of Parliament.

- When using cases you will not need to refer to the date of the case and with complicated case names it is sufficient to use a shortened simplified version – examiners will know which case you mean. Criminal cases are usually written *R v*, but in most AS Law textbooks (and this Revision Guide) cases are referred to just by the name of the defendant (e.g. *Cunningham, Miller*).

- When referring to an Act of Parliament, you must include the date of the Act as well.

1 Parliamentary law making

For this topic you need to understand:

- the influences on Parliament and their advantages and disadvantages
- the process by which Parliament consults with people and then introduces and passes legislation
- the roles of the House of Commons, the House of Lords and the Crown and the advantages and disadvantages of the parliamentary process
- the idea of parliamentary supremacy and its limitations.

Influences on Parliament
Revised

- **Parliament** is the supreme law-making body in the United Kingdom. Pressure on Parliament to make or reform the law comes from a number of sources.
- In practice most of the laws Parliament passes are drawn up by the **Government**, which is elected to govern the country. When a general election is to be held, each political party presents a party manifesto, setting out its proposals for new legislation and these ideas, together with the other things that all governments need to do in order to run the country, are the main influence on the laws that Parliament passes.
- The Government also has to respond to unexpected events like the threat from terrorism and it sometimes has to introduce laws to comply with new European Union regulations. All of these are political influences and we would expect them to play an important part in influencing what Parliament does.

> **Key terms**
>
> Parliament is sometimes referred to as the legislature – the law-making body. The Government is sometimes referred to as the executive and it is the body that runs the country and implements the law.

Pressure groups
Revised

Pressure groups are bodies of people with a shared interest in getting the government to change the law in certain areas. There are many different kinds:

- **Sectional** or **interest** groups exist to further the ends of their own particular section of society. Examples are trade unions, groups such as the National Farmers' Union (NFU) and professional associations like the British Medical Association, which represents doctors.
- **Cause groups** are those that promote a particular idea or belief. Examples include environmental groups like Greenpeace and Friends of the Earth and groups like Amnesty International, which campaigns on human rights.
- Another distinction is between **insider groups** that have direct contact with government ministers and Parliament (as many of the sectional groups do) and **outsider groups** like Fathers4Justice who have to resort to direct action to promote their cause.

Exam practice answers and quick quizzes at **www.therevisionbutton.co.uk/myrevisionnotes**

- Sometimes a pressure group is set up as a result of a tragic event. The Snowdrop Campaign, organised after the Dunblane massacre in 1996, resulted in Parliament banning the private ownership of most types of handguns.

- The degree of influence exercised by such groups varies.

- Professional associations representing groups such as lawyers and doctors, made up of well-educated, articulate and often wealthy individuals, are influential. Governments of all parties tend to consult them before introducing a Bill affecting their interests. The ban on smoking in public places in July 2007 was partly the result of lobbying by the British Medical Association.

- Outsider groups often have to resort to publicity stunts (such as those carried out by Fathers4Justice) or marches and demonstrations, but most pressure groups engage in lobbying, produce promotional literature, organise petitions and generally try to gain as much publicity as possible for their cause. An example of a very successful campaign by outsider groups is that by Stonewall and other gay rights groups, which resulted in Parliament passing the Civil Partnership Act in 2004, and approving gay marriage in 2012.

- Large groups are often more successful than smaller ones, but sometimes one person can bring about change almost single-handedly. The late Mary Whitehouse headed a campaign against child pornography, which led the government to introduce the Protection of Children Act 1984, and more recently Jamie Oliver was successful in promoting healthier meals in schools.

Exam tip

When discussing an influence you should explain the importance of the influence on law making. This is best done by referring to examples of actual statutes.

Advantages of pressure groups

- Pressure groups give the public and particularly minorities a voice. They act as a safety valve for frustrations, as in pro-hunting and anti-Iraq War protests.

- They help MPs keep in touch with what people think. For example, pressure from environmental groups may have persuaded the government to change car tax regulations to favour smaller, more fuel-efficient cars and pressure from the anti-smoking group ASH and doctors' groups led to the ban on smoking in public places in 2007.

- Pressure groups raise public awareness of issues. For example, Fathers4Justice has been successful through a variety of stunts in raising awareness of the plight of fathers denied access to their children after a divorce.

- Members of pressure groups often have considerable expertise and can therefore suggest detailed and well-thought-out law changes. Many groups have draft Bills ready for backbench MPs to introduce.

Disadvantages of pressure groups

- Some large pressure groups that represent powerful organisations are extremely influential, and it is difficult for smaller pressure groups to match their influence.

- Environmental groups claim that the strength of the road lobby and the airline industry means that new roads or airport extensions are difficult to fight.

- The methods of some pressure groups can be a problem, for example strikes and protests such as the blockading of oil depots can cause

Exam tip

If you are asked about advantages or disadvantages of influences, you should try and explain why the particular point is an advantage or disadvantage and also provide some evidence or examples.

disruption. The direct action tactics of Fathers4Justice have been criticised. Members of the Countryside Alliance broke into the House of Commons as part of its campaign in favour of fox hunting.

- Pressure groups may only represent a minority view when they are successful in changing the law, as was arguably the case when the death penalty was abolished in 1966.

The media

- The media includes television, radio, newspapers and journals and they play a powerful role in bringing issues to the attention of the government.
- Newspapers in particular promote specific issues or causes. For example, the *Daily Mail* has often run headlines on immigration or asylum issues in order to try to achieve tighter controls, and the *Sun* has consistently campaigned against what it sees as the growing influence of the EU on British life.
- Another example of media influence was the campaign run by the now defunct *News of the World* in 2000 following the murder of Sarah Payne by a paedophile. It published details of known paedophiles in order to force the government to take action. The result was a register of sex offenders and the promise of much closer supervision of those released into the community.
- Investigative journalism can also be influential. For example TV programmes like *Panorama* have often drawn attention to abuses or scandals and the *Daily Telegraph* played an important part in bringing about reform of the expenses rules when it published details in 2009 showing what expenses some MPs were claiming.

Advantages of the media

- The media play a powerful role in bringing issues to the attention of Parliament or the government and can force it to act. Examples are the publication in 2009 of MPs' expenses claims by the *Daily Telegraph* and the campaign by the *News of the World* in 2000, which resulted in a register of sex offenders.
- Coverage in newspapers and on television and radio can raise the public profile of an issue and add weight to public opinion.

> **Exam tip**
>
> Questions on influences will sometimes allow you to choose which one you want to talk about, but they may also specify particular influences, so you need to be prepared for this.

Disadvantages of the media

- It is a concern that ownership of British newspapers and other branches of the media is in the hands of a relatively small number of individuals.
- Newspapers often adopt views that reflect those of their owners. Rupert Murdoch, who owns the *Sun*, *The Times*, the *Sunday Times* and Sky television, has used his newspapers to project his own views, particularly his strong opposition to the EU.
- Concern has also been expressed about links between the media and politicians. For example the appointment of Andy Coulson, the former *News of the World* editor, as David Cameron's director of communications in 2007 and the social contacts between David Cameron and Rebekah Brooks when she was editor of the *News of the World*.
- The media have a tendency to create panics by drawing attention to and often exaggerating issues, such as the activities of paedophiles. The

media may sometimes whip up public opinion, which can result in unwise legislation, as was arguably the case with the Dangerous Dogs Act 1991.

The Law Commission

Revised

- Established by the Law Commission Act 1965, it is a full-time body with five Commissioners. The chairperson is a High Court judge and the other four are from the legal professions and academic lawyers. All members of staff are legally trained.
- The Commission's work involves looking at reform of the law, codification and consolidation.
- The Commission may have topics referred to it by government departments, or may select a topic of its own, which will be considered after government approval has been gained.
- When proposing reform of an area of law, the Commission produces an initial consultative paper and then a final report, setting out recommendations and sometimes a draft Bill. Legislation that has resulted from this process includes the Law Reform (Year and a Day Rule) Act 1996 and the Contract (Rights of Third Parties) Act 1999.
- The Commission also recommends the repeal of obsolete Statutes. In 2012 it recommended the repeal of nearly 800 old laws.
- Another aim is to codify the law in certain areas, but this has not been achieved. The Draft Criminal Code was published in 1985 but has never become law. More recently the Commission has selected areas of law and clarified them, hoping to codify them at a later date if possible. The Land Registration Act 2002 and the Fraud Act 2006 are examples of areas of law reformed in this way.
- Consolidation involves drawing together all the provisions set out in a number of statutes, so that they are all in one Act. About five consolidation Bills are produced each year. The Powers of the Criminal Courts (Sentencing) Act 2000 was changed by the Criminal Justice and Courts Act 2000, where community sentences were renamed and new powers of sentencing created.

> **Exam tip**
>
> Notice that the role of the Law Commission is to recommend changes in the law, but it is dependent on Parliament implementing its proposals.

Advantages of the Law Commission

- It is a permanent, full-time body and can investigate any area of law it believes to be in need of reform.
- It produces draft Bills ready for Parliament to introduce, which reduces the workload for ministers.
- It has been responsible for many sensible changes to the law, for example the Unfair Contract Terms Act 1977, the Fraud Act 2006 and the abolition of the 'Year and a Day' rule.
- It can undertake extensive research and engage in wide consultation, so its recommendations for law reform are well informed and this helps to avoid problems in the application of the law.

Disadvantages of the Law Commission

- Parliament has often ignored the Commission's proposals.
- Up until 1999, only two-thirds of its proposals had been implemented. Often this is because governments cannot find time in the legislative programme for non-urgent law reform. A good example is reform of

the law on non-fatal offences. This was recommended by the Law Commission in a report in 1993 and accepted by the New Labour government of 1997 who produced a draft Bill in 1998, but they never implemented it.

- The Law Commission investigates as many as 20–30 areas at the same time. This may mean that each investigation is not as thorough as one carried out by a Royal Commission or a Commission of Inquiry.

Now test yourself 1

1 What is the purpose of a party manifesto?
2 What are insider groups?
3 What statute resulted from campaigning by Stonewall and other gay rights groups?
4 Give an example of a sectional or interest group.
5 What does the media include?
6 Give an example of the media bringing an issue to the attention of Parliament.
7 Give an example of unwise legislation resulting from the media whipping up public opinion.
8 When was the Law Commission set up?
9 What does the Law Commission's work involve?
10 Give an example of a Law Commission proposal that was never implemented.

Answers on p.126

The legislative process

- UK legislation consists of Acts of Parliament, which are also known as statutes. Legislation is the result of a process involving the House of Commons, the House of Lords and the monarch (the Queen).
- Statutes are referred to as **primary legislation**.
- Most legislation is drawn up (drafted) by the government.
- The House of Commons is made up of Members of Parliament (MPs), elected to represent the people in their individual local constituencies.
- The political party with the majority of seats forms the government of the day.
- The House of Lords, which is unelected, consists of hereditary peers, life peers appointed because of their contribution to society or politics, and senior bishops.

How statutes are created

- All Acts of Parliament begin life as Bills. Before a Bill is drawn up the government department involved in the proposed changes to the law may issue a consultative document known as a **Green Paper**, setting out ideas for legislation and allowing interested parties to comment on them.
- Any necessary changes can then be made and the final proposals set out in a **White Paper**. For example, the Court and Legal Services Act 1990 was preceded by three Green Papers published in January 1989 and a White Paper ('Legal services: a framework for the future') published in July 1989, which set out the then government's proposals in relation to legal services generally.

Exam tip

Green and White Papers are not part of the parliamentary process itself because they precede the drafting of the Bill and reference to them will not usually be credited in a question about the process in Parliament or in one about the process in either of the two Houses.

Green and White Papers would be relevant in a more general question about the making of an Act of Parliament.

Types of Bill

- **Public Bills** are by far the most common type and can be subdivided into Government Bills and Private Members' Bills.

- **Government Bills** are introduced and piloted through the parliamentary process by a government minister. Some are controversial and reflect the views of the political party in power, such as the Bills to privatise public utilities under the Conservative governments of Margaret Thatcher and John Major. Others are concerned simply with the smooth running of the country, such as the Access to Justice Act 1999. There are some 35 to 40 Government Bills each year, most of which become law.

- **Private Members' Bills** are introduced by backbench MPs, whose names have been selected by ballot (20 each year).

- To be successful, a Private Members' Bill needs to have the tacit support of the government of the day. A good example is the Abortion Act 1967, which resulted from David Steel's Private Members' Bill and with which the Labour government sympathised. Other examples of Private Members' Bills that have become law include the Murder (Abolition of Death Penalty) Act 1965, the Marriage Act 1994, which allowed buildings other than register offices or places of worship to be used to conduct marriages, and the Computer Misuse Act 1990.

- **Private Bills** are usually put forward by a local authority, public corporation or large public company and only affect the bodies concerned. An example is the Medway Council Act 2004, which gave Medway Council more power to control street trading in the borough.

- There are also **Hybrid Bills**, which, when they become statutes, alter the general law but particularly affect the legal rights of a small number of people. The Channel Tunnel Act 1987 and the Crossrail Act 2008 are good examples. Both cases are major transport projects that would have significant impact on local people. Another example is the HS2 Bill published in November 2013.

Key terms

Public Bills are those that affect the whole country; private Bills affect only specific individuals, organisations or areas.

Process of a Bill through Parliament

- A Bill cannot become an Act of Parliament until it has been passed by both Houses of Parliament. The procedure consists of a number of stages and may commence in either the House of Commons or the House of Lords, although finance Bills must begin in the House of Commons.

- The **First reading** takes place when the title of the Bill is read out to the House.

- The **Second reading** is the crucial stage, in which the House holds a full debate on the main principles of the Bill. At the end of the debate, a vote is taken as to whether the Bill should proceed further.

- If the vote is in favour, the Bill passes to the **Committee stage**. This involves a detailed examination of each clause of the Bill by a standing committee of between 16 and 50 MPs. They will probably propose amendments to various clauses of the Bill.

- The **Report stage** is when the committee reports back to the House on any amendments that have been made. These are debated and voted on.

- At the **Third reading** the Bill is presented again to the House and the final vote is taken.

Exam tip

In a question on the formal process of law-making or the stages through which a Bill passes, you should mention that it has to go through both Houses of Parliament.

- If the Bill was introduced in the House of Commons, it then passes to the House of Lords (or vice versa), where the same procedure is repeated.

- If the House of Lords makes amendments to a Bill that has already passed through the House of Commons, the Bill is referred back to the Commons to consider the amendments.

- Once a Bill has passed successfully through all the stages in both Houses, it has to receive formal consent of the monarch in order to become law. This is known as the **Royal Assent**.

- Some Acts of Parliament come into force when Royal Assent is given, but most start on a specific date, which may be stated in the Act.

Process of Parliament

Revised ☐

Parliament consists of the House of Commons, the House of Lords and the Crown.

Role of the House of Commons

- Because the House of Commons is an elected body, it has the most important role in the law-making process. All important legislation begins in the House of Commons and all finance Bills must start there.

- By using the Parliament Acts, the Commons can defeat any attempt by the Lords to oppose a measure that the Commons has passed. In practice, this power is rarely used and the Commons often has to compromise in order to get legislation through.

- Because the Lords can delay a Bill for a year, it has considerably more influence over the Commons during the last year of a parliament's life.

Role of the House of Lords

- Bills can start life in the House of Lords, though most begin in the Commons. Usually legislation that starts in the Lords is not politically controversial or has a legal subject matter, for example the Access to Justice Act 1999.

- However, the House of Lords is primarily a revising and debating chamber and it allows further detailed scrutiny of Bills that have already passed through the House of Commons.

- At times, the House of Lords has made the government rethink its proposals. For example, in March 2005 it forced the government to amend its plans in the Terrorism Bill for control orders to deal with terrorist suspects.

- The unelected House of Lords used to be able to prevent legislation put forward by the elected House of Commons, as the agreement of both Houses was necessary. This power is restricted by the Parliament Acts 1911 and 1949. If the House of Lords reject a Bill, it can still become law, provided it is reintroduced to the House of Commons in the next parliamentary session and passes all the stages again. The Lords are not allowed to delay finance Bills.

- This power to force the Lords to pass a Bill has only been used five times, for example to push through the War Crimes Act 1991 and the Hunting Act 2004.

> **Exam tip**
>
> If a question asks about the role of the House of Lords you should make sure that you refer to how conflicts with the House of Commons are resolved.

Role of the Crown

- The Crown plays a purely formal role and any attempt by a monarch to thwart the will of the Commons and Lords would not be tolerated. Since Queen Anne refused to pass the Scotch Militia Bill 1707, no monarch has refused to assent to a Bill.

Exam tip

While the role of the Crown is purely formal and should be mentioned quite briefly in an answer, the House of Lords has a number of roles and should be discussed in more detail. The role of the Commons should be emphasised as the most important.

Advantages and disadvantages of the parliamentary process

Revised

Advantages

- The process is **democratic** because the House of Commons is elected, MPs are answerable to the voters and there must be an election at least every five years. The Commons can, if necessary, force its will on the Lords by using the Parliament Acts.

- Parliament takes note of public opinion. The vote in February 2006 for a complete ban on smoking in public places could be seen as Parliament responding to public opinion.

- The House of Lords is a useful check. There are many people in the Lords who have specialist expertise, for example lawyers, doctors and scientists, or who have been successful in running companies or charities. These people bring practical knowledge and experience to their examination of Bills.

- The legislative process is thorough, with detailed committee examination of Bills in both Houses as well as general debates.

- When it is necessary, an Act can be passed quickly. For example, the Criminal Justice (Terrorism and Conspiracy) Act 1998 went through all its stages in two days, and the Northern Ireland Act 1972 was passed in just 24 hours.

Exam tip

When explaining why a particular point is an advantage or disadvantage, try to refer to some examples.

Disadvantages

- There is not enough time to pass all the legislation that is necessary and Reform Bills (e.g. to modernise the law on non-fatal offences) are often left out of the government's legislative programme.

- There is inadequate scrutiny of legislation. The government controls the parliamentary timetable and through processes such as the guillotine it can restrict discussion of a Bill. Because the government has a majority on all the standing committees, it is able to defeat any amendments put forward in committee.

- Some Bills are passed too quickly, usually in response to a real or imagined emergency. The Dangerous Dogs Act 1991 was described in one case as 'an ill-thought-out piece of legislation', passed with too much haste.

- The House of Lords, which is not elected, is able to delay legislation that the House of Commons has passed. No other democratic country has an unelected second chamber able to frustrate the decisions of an elected body in this way.

- The House of Commons is not a truly independent body. In most cases, it does what the government tells it to do, because a majority of MPs are members of the governing party and pressured by the whips into supporting government Bills.

Doctrine of parliamentary supremacy

- **Parliamentary supremacy** (sovereignty) is the idea, proposed by Dicey in 1885, that as a democratically elected body, Parliament is the supreme law-making body in the country.

- The main elements are that 'Parliament … has … under the English constitution, the right to make or unmake any law whatever … and that no person or body is recognised by the law of England as having a right to override or set aside the legislation of Parliament.'

- This means that Acts of Parliament passed using the proper procedures cannot be challenged. They must be applied by the courts and override any judicial precedent, delegated legislation or previous Act of Parliament that covers that area of law. Parliament also has the power to rescind (unmake) any law it has passed.

- No parliament can bind its successors (i.e. no parliament can make laws that will restrict law making in future parliaments).

Limitations on sovereignty

- **Entrenched laws** deal with fundamental constitutional issues and are difficult for any future parliament to change, for example legislation extending voting rights to women and lowering the voting age to 18. Another example is the more recent granting of legislative powers to a Scottish Parliament.

- Membership of the European Union (EU) takes priority over conflicting laws in member states. The European Communities Act 1972 incorporates this principle into UK law.

- Even if Parliament passes an Act that conflicts with EU law, EU law must prevail, as shown in the *Factortame* case in 1990. For areas of law not covered by the EU, Parliament is supreme.

- The Human Rights Act 1998 incorporates the European Convention on Human Rights into English law. Under the Act, the Convention does not have superiority over English law and Parliament can still make laws that conflict with it.

- But under s. 3 of the Act, the courts are required as far as possible to interpret Acts so that they comply with the Convention.

- If an Act cannot be reconciled with the Convention, a judge can make a declaration of incompatibility, although ministers are not obliged to change the law. Although Parliament could refuse to respond to such a declaration, in practice it is likely that a government will accept that the legislation has to change, as happened following the declaration of incompatibility in *A and others v Secretary of State for the Home Department (2004)*.

Key terms

Parliamentary supremacy is sometimes referred to as parliamentary sovereignty. It means that Parliament is the supreme law-making body in the country and its enactments have to be obeyed by everyone.

Exam tip

A question might refer to either the sovereignty or to the supremacy of parliament. You would answer both in the same way, explaining first what the term means and then identifying the characteristics that illustrate it.

Exam tip

A question may ask you to refer to just one limitation. Choose one that you feel you can say the most about.

Now test yourself 2

1 What is a Green Paper?
2 Give an example of a Private Members' Bill.
3 In which stage in the passage of a Bill through Parliament is a full debate held?
4 What can the Commons use to defeat an attempt by the Lords to oppose a measure that the Commons has passed?
5 Give an example of a Statute that started in the House of Lords.
6 When was the last time that a monarch refused to sign a Bill?
7 Which Act was passed by Parliament in just 24 hours?
8 What is parliamentary supremacy?
9 What is meant by Parliament not binding its successors?
10 Give an example of a case in which judges made a declaration of incompatibility.

Answers on p.126

Check your understanding

1 In the table below briefly explain two advantages and two disadvantages of each influence on Parliament.

Advantages of Law Commission	1 2	
Disadvantages of Law Commission	1 2	
Advantages of pressure groups	1 2	
Disadvantages of pressure groups	1 2	
Advantages of the media	1 2	
Disadvantages of the media	1 2	

2 For a Bill starting in the House of Commons briefly summarise in the table below what happens at each stage.

First reading	
Second reading	
Committee stage	
Report stage	
Third reading	
House of Lords	
Royal Assent	

Answers on p.126

Exam practice

1 Explain what is meant by parliamentary supremacy and outline one limitation on it. [10 marks]
2 Outline the law-making process in Parliament. [10 marks]
3 Discuss the advantages of parliamentary law making. [10 marks + 2 marks AO3]

Online

Exam summary

- In the exam you could be asked about influences on Parliament. Make sure you learn about pressure groups, the media *and* the Law Commission, as you may not be given a choice from which to choose.

- Remember that each of these influences try to affect decisions made by Parliament, so the best evidence you can give will be an example of their influence on legislation that is passed.

- You may be asked about the advantages and disadvantages of an influence. Prepare at least three on each one.

- To answer a question on the parliamentary process you will need to know the stages in both the Commons and the Lords.

- You could be asked a question about something very specific, for example Green or White Papers.

- Make sure you know about and can distinguish the roles of the House of Commons, the House of Lords and the Crown.

- You could be asked about the advantages and disadvantages of the parliamentary process. Prepare at least three of each.

- There may be a question on the supremacy of Parliament; only include limitations if the question specifically asks you to.

Exam practice answers and quick quizzes at **www.therevisionbutton.co.uk/myrevisionnotes**

2 Delegated legislation

For this topic you need to understand:

- what is meant by delegated legislation
- the various types delegated legislation
- the parliamentary and judicial controls on delegated legislation
- the reasons for and advantages and disadvantages of delegated legislation.

Delegated legislation
Revised

- Delegated legislation (secondary legislation) is law that is not made by Parliament but under its authority. Authority (permission) is usually given in a 'parent' Act of Parliament known as an **enabling Act**. This Act creates the framework of the law and then delegates power to others to make more detailed law in that area.
- Examples of enabling Acts are the Local Government Act 1972, which allows local authorities such as district and county councils to make by-laws, and the Access to Justice Act 1999, which gives the Lord Chancellor wide powers to alter aspects of the system of state funding for legal cases.

> **Key terms**
>
> Delegated Legislation is legislation passed by bodies other than Parliament, but with the permission of Parliament.

Types of delegated legislation
Revised

Orders in Council

- Orders in Council are made by the Queen and Privy Council and can be used for a wide variety of purposes, for example the regulation of certain professional bodies.
- They are used when an ordinary statutory instrument would be inappropriate, for instance when transferring responsibilities between government departments.
- Orders in Council were used to transfer powers from ministers of the UK government to ministers of the devolved assemblies in Scotland and Wales.
- They are used to dissolve Parliament in preparation for a General Election and sometimes to make specific law changes, as under the Misuse of Drugs Act 1971 to reclassify cannabis. They are also used to give effect to European directives under s. 2(2) of the European Communities Act 1972.
- In times of emergency, when Parliament is not sitting, an Order in Council can be made under the Emergency Powers Act 1920 and the Civil Contingencies Act 2004. These powers were used during the foot-and-mouth crisis in 2001, when decisions needed to be made quickly to try to prevent the spread of the disease. They were also used during the fuel crisis of 2000.

> **Exam tip**
>
> You will almost certainly be asked to describe at least one type of delegated legislation. Often the type(s) will be specified. You need to be confident that you can describe all three types, with suitable examples.

Statutory Instruments

- This is the most common type of delegated legislation. There were 3117 Statutory Instruments made in 2011.

- Authority is given to ministers and government departments to make detailed regulations for their area of responsibility, for example the Minister of Transport has the power under various Road Traffic Acts to make detailed road traffic regulations. Under the terms of the Road Traffic Act 1998, the Traffic Signs Regulations 2002 were made which regulate the size and colour of road signs.

- Regulations are a good way of updating primary legislation and adapting the law to changing circumstances. For example, the Health and Safety at Work Act 1974 has been updated through the Management of Health and Safety at Work Regulations 1992.

- Statutory Instruments are used to implement European Union directives in English law. An example is the Unfair Terms in Consumer Contracts Regulations 1994, which implemented a directive aimed at giving greater protection to consumers.

- They are also used to bring an Act of Parliament, or parts of it, into effect by means of a Commencement Order. For example, the Equality Act 2010 was brought into effect in stages by five Commencement Orders.

> **Typical mistake**
> Students often confuse Orders in Council with statutory instruments. You need to learn the points for each separately and make sure you know the differences.

By-laws

- Parliament has given local authorities and other public bodies the right to make law in certain areas.

- Local authorities, such as county councils, district councils and parish councils, can make by-laws to cover such things as parking restrictions and banning the drinking of alcohol in certain public places.

- Under s. 19 of the Public Libraries and Museums Act 1964, Cornwall County Council made by-laws about the use of libraries in the county. The introduction of the congestion charge zone in central London is another example.

- Public corporations and certain companies can also make by-laws to help to enforce rules concerning public behaviour; the London Underground's ban on smoking is an example. Another example is the National Trust Act 1907, under which the National Trust has the power to make by-laws affecting National Trust property.

- All by-laws must be approved by the relevant government minister.

- Professional regulations also come under delegated legislation, such as those found in the Solicitors Act 1974 empowering the Law Society to regulate the conduct of its members.

> **Exam tip**
> It is a good idea to have examples of by-laws from your own local area which you can use in your exam answer.

Control over delegated legislation

Revised

- Statistically, far more delegated legislation is made each year than primary legislation. A great deal of legislation is therefore being made by persons and bodies other than Parliament, without being subject to the full scrutiny of the parliamentary process.

- Because most delegated legislation is not made by elected bodies and many people have the power to create it, it is important to make sure that the power is not abused and is controlled. This can be done by Parliament or the Judiciary (the courts).

Control by Parliament

- Parliament has some control at the time an enabling Act is made, as it sets the limits for making delegated legislation under that Act.

- In addition, the Delegated Powers Scrutiny Committee in the House of Lords can decide whether the provisions in a Bill to delegate legislative power are inappropriate. Its report is presented to the House of Lords before the committee stage but it has no power to amend the Bill.

- Some enabling Acts require an **affirmative resolution** from Parliament before the delegated legislation can become law. The delegated legislation has to be laid before both Houses and it only becomes law if a vote to approve it is taken within a specified time. For example, under the Criminal Justice and Public Order Act 1994 the minister is allowed to make regulations to control sales by ticket touts at sporting events but only if such regulations are specifically approved by Parliament. Under the Hunting Act 2004, the minister may allow hunting with dogs in some circumstances as long as Parliament consents.

- Much more delegated legislation is subject to a **negative resolution**. The delegated legislation is put before Parliament and if no member has put down a motion to annul it within a specified period (usually 40 days) it becomes law.

- The **Joint Committee on Statutory Instruments**, with members from both Houses of Parliament (the Scrutiny Committee), reviews all Statutory Instruments and can draw the attention of Parliament to any that need special consideration. The Committee has no power to alter the legislation as it merely reports back on its findings, but it does provide a check on delegated legislation.

- Parliament itself holds the ultimate safeguard, in that it can withdraw the delegated power and revoke any piece of delegated legislation at any time.

Control by the judiciary

- Unlike a Statute, the validity of delegated legislation can be challenged in the courts. Any individual who has a personal interest in the delegated legislation (i.e. who is affected by it) may apply to the courts under the **judicial review** procedure.

- The delegated legislation will be invalid if it is **ultra vires** (goes beyond the powers granted by Parliament). If it is found to be **ultra vires**, the delegated legislation is declared void and ineffective.

- This can be in the form of **procedural *ultra vires***, where a public authority has not followed the procedures set out in the enabling Act for creating delegated legislation. In *Agricultural, Horticultural and Forestry Training Board v Aylesbury Mushrooms Ltd (1972)*, failure by the Minister of Labour to consult interested parties as required by the Act led to the order being declared invalid.

- A claim of **substantive *ultra vires*** occurs where the delegated legislation goes beyond the powers granted by the enabling Act. In *AG v Fulham Corporation (1921)* an Act allowed local authorities to set up clothes

> **Typical mistake**
>
> Students often confuse parliamentary and judicial controls and write about the wrong one in the exam. Parliamentary controls are those which Parliament has over the making and repeal of delegated legislation. Judicial controls are those exercised by the judges in the courts when people challenge the validity of a particular piece of delegated legislation.

washing facilities for people to use, but the Corporation set up a laundry to do people's washing for them and therefore went beyond its powers.

- A decision may also be considered **unreasonable**. This may be because the rules are unjust, are made in bad faith or are so perverse that no reasonable person would have made them. In *Strickland v Hayes (1896)* a by-law prohibiting the singing of obscene songs was too widely drawn so that it prohibited the singing of such songs in private as well as in public and was therefore unreasonable.

Advantages and disadvantages of delegated legislation

Revised

Advantages

- It saves Parliament's time. There is not enough time for Parliament to consider every detail of every regulation and rule. Delegated legislation frees Parliament to concentrate on broad issues of policy rather than masses of detail. More than 3000 Statutory Instruments are passed every year. For example, the Road Traffic Act 1972 provided that motor cyclists had to wear helmets, but the details were left to the minister to publish in the Motor Cycles (Protective Helmets) Regulations 1980.

- Parliament does not have the knowledge or technical expertise necessary in certain areas, such as building regulations or health and safety regulations at work. Delegated legislation allows the use of experts in the relevant areas to make the rules, as for example in drawing up the Air Navigation Order 1995 which contains complex technical regulations about civil aviation.

- Local people know local needs. As a result, local authority by-laws are often more appropriate than broad and general national legislation. For example, Cornwall County Council was the best authority to make rules for libraries in Cornwall under the Public Libraries and Museums Act 1964.

- Delegated legislation can be achieved more quickly than an Act of Parliament. It can also be amended more quickly if circumstances change, allowing flexibility. Orders in Council can be used in emergencies when Parliament is not sitting, for example during the foot-and-mouth crisis of 2001.

- Delegated legislation is easily revoked if it causes problems. An Act of Parliament requires another Statute to amend or revoke it, which takes much longer.

Exam tip

Some exam questions ask about the reasons for delegated legislation rather than the advantages of it. The same points can be made, but your answer needs to be worded so that it refers to reasons.

Disadvantages

- The main argument against delegated legislation is that it is undemocratic, because much of it is made by unelected people rather than by Parliament.

- Much delegated legislation is then sub-delegated and made by civil servants in the relevant government departments rather than by the ministers who were originally given the delegated powers.

- Civil servants are unaccountable to the electorate. (This is not the case with by-laws, as local authorities are elected bodies and accountable to the voters in their area.)

- The large amount of delegated legislation makes it difficult to keep track of the current law (in 2011, 3117 Statutory Instruments were made).

- There is little publicity compared to that received by Acts of Parliament, so people may be unaware that a particular piece of legislation exists.

- Control is not always effective. Few Statutory Instruments have affirmative resolution and MPs are too busy to look at the others.
- The powers of the Scrutiny Committee are limited, as it can only consider whether the delegated powers have been used correctly and not the merits of the legislation. Its reports are not binding either.
- There are also limitations on judicial control. The delegated legislation may have been in force for years before someone affected by it is prepared to challenge it.

> **Exam tip**
>
> In a question about the advantages or disadvantages of delegated legislation, try to refer to examples or evidence to support your points.

Now test yourself 1

Tested

1 What is an enabling Act?
2 Give an example of an enabling Act.
3 Who makes Orders in Council?
4 Give an example of detailed regulations made by statutory instrument.
5 Who has to approve all by-laws?
6 What is required for a Statutory Instrument requiring affirmative resolution to become law?
7 What does the Joint Committee on Statutory Instruments do?
8 What is procedural *ultra vires*?
9 Give a case example of substantive *ultra vires*.
10 Give an example of delegated legislation using expert knowledge to make technical regulations.
11 Give an example of Orders in Council being used in an emergency.
12 What is meant by sub-delegation?

Answers on p.127

Check your understanding

1 Fill in the missing information on controls by Parliament and controls by the Judiciary.

Controls by Parliament
Parliament can set _____ in the E_____ A_____.
There are two C _____. The first is_____.
The second is _____.
A _____ R_____. This is where_____.
Example: _____.
N_____ R_____. This is where _____.
It is used for most S _____ I_____.
Parliament can r _____ the E_____ A_____.

Controls by the Judiciary

An action can be brought for J_____ R_____ in the H_____

C_____ and the court can decide that the DL is u_____ v_____.

This means that the body making it has gone b_____ its p_____.

S_____ u_____ v_____. This is where the body making the DL did not

have the a_____ in the E_____ A_____ for doing this.

An example is _____.

P_____ u_____ v_____. This is where the body making the

DL has not _____.

An example is _____.

The courts might decide that a piece of DL is u_____.

An example is: _____.

2 Develop each of the points in the table below, explaining why each is a reason for having delegated legislation.

Saves Parliament's time	
Technical expertise	
Local needs	
Speed	
Easily revoked	

Answers on p.127

Answers on p.127

Exam practice

1 Explain what is meant by by-laws and Orders in Council. **[10 marks]**

2 Describe judicial controls on delegated legislation. **[10 marks]**

3 Discuss the disadvantages of delegated legislation. **[10 marks + 2 marks AO3]**

Online

Exam summary

✔ You are likely to be asked about one or more of the types of delegated legislation: Statutory Instruments, Orders in Council and by-laws.

✔ You must know who makes each type of delegated legislation and be able to give examples of different uses. Don't forget to mention the authority under which it is made.

✔ You need to know about parliamentary and judicial controls – don't mix them up.

✔ You might be asked about reasons for delegated legislation. Remember that they are the same as advantages, but you need to word your answer differently.

✔ You are likely to be asked to discuss the advantages and disadvantages of delegated legislation, so prepare at least three of each.

3 Statutory interpretation

For this topic you need to understand:

- the process of statutory interpretation is used by judges in the courts when there is a dispute or uncertainty over the meaning of a word or phrase in an Act of Parliament or piece of delegated legislation
- the role of the courts is to find out how Parliament intended the law to apply and to carry out this interpretation
- the various aids and rules of language available to help judges interpret statutes, including internal and external aids and rules of language
- the rules of interpretation and their advantages and disadvantages: common law approaches (literal, golden and mischief rules) and purposive approach.

Aids to statutory interpretation

Internal or intrinsic aids

- These are found in the Act itself and may help to make its meaning clear.
- The **long title** and the **short title of the Act**: in *Cornwall County Council v Baker* (2003), the Divisional Court referred to the long title to confirm the purpose of the Protection of Animals (Amendment) Act 2000.
- The **preamble** (if there is one): older Acts have a detailed preamble outlining what the statute covered and its purpose.
- **Marginal notes** and headings: some sections of the Act may have headings and marginal notes are usually added by the person drafting the Act. Both may provide guidance.
- A marginal note was referred to in *R v Tivnan* (1999) in order to clarify whether it was Parliament's intention to deprive drug dealers of assets equivalent in value to the proceeds obtained from drug dealing, and not necessarily just those assets purchased directly from the proceeds of the drug dealing.
- Most Acts now contain **interpretation sections**. An example is s. 10 of the Theft Act 1968, which, after referring to the use of 'a weapon of offence' in aggravated burglary, defines it as 'any article made or adapted for use for causing injury'.
- Acts often contain **schedules**, which are found at the end of an Act and include more detailed clarification. An example is Schedule 2 of the Unfair Contract Terms Act 1977, which outlines the tests for determining the principle of reasonableness.

> **Exam tip**
>
> Exam questions frequently ask about aids, but check carefully to see whether you are being asked about internal, external or both. Remember too that aids may be linked with something else such as rules of language or one of the rules of interpretation.

> **Key terms**
>
> Intrinsic means inside the Act; extrinsic means outside the Act.

Advantages of internal aids

- It is more respectful of Parliament to look elsewhere in the Act rather than outside the Act.
- It is quick and easy to look at things like marginal notes, which were helpful in *Tivnan*, or at the long title (used in *Cornwall CC v Baker*).
- Some internal aids like interpretation sections and Schedules are designed to provide definitions and explanations, so it is common sense to look at them. For example s. 10 of the Theft Act explained the meaning of 'weapon of offence'.

Disadvantages of internal aids

- Most problems with wording are not likely to be solved by looking elsewhere in the Act, especially if the words are ambiguous as in *Allen* or very plain but wrong as in *Whitely v Chappell (1868)*.
- Internal aids alone are unlikely to be sufficient and if judges were not allowed to refer to anything outside the Act it would be more difficult for them to avoid unfair or absurd decisions.

External or extrinsic aids

These are found outside the Act and include the following:

- **Dictionaries** of various kinds: for example, in *Vaughan v Vaughan (1973)* a man had been pestering his ex-wife and the Court of Appeal used a dictionary in order to define 'molest' and concluded that the definition was wide enough to cover his behaviour. Another example is *Cheeseman (1990)*, where a dictionary was used to decide the meaning of the word 'passengers'.
- **Previous Acts of Parliament and earlier case law**: in *Royal Crown Derby Porcelain Co. Ltd v Raymond Russell (1949)*, when considering the Rent and Mortgage Act 1933, the court interpreted words used in the Act by referring to similar words used in an earlier Act and to the interpretation applied to these words in a number of cases.
- **Reference to Hansard** (the official report of the proceedings in Parliament): until 1990, the courts were not allowed to refer to Hansard in order to find out Parliament's intention. This was overturned in *Pepper v Hart (1993)*. However, this use is restricted to cases where the words of an Act are ambiguous or obscure or lead to an absurdity, and even then, only where there is a clear statement by the minister introducing the legislation that would resolve the doubt.
- The wider use of Hansard is only permitted if the legislation in question has introduced an international convention or European directive into English law.
- **Law reform reports** from bodies such as the Law Commission.
- **International treaties**: *Fothergill v Monarch Airlines Ltd (1980)* confirmed that background working papers could be used to ascertain the meaning of an ambiguous or doubtful section of an Act based on an international treaty.
- **Explanatory notes**: since 1999, all government Bills are accompanied by explanatory notes, which provide guidance on complex parts of the Bill.

> **Typical mistake**
>
> Students sometimes confuse internal and external aids. Make sure that you learn each separately and are clear about their characteristics.

Advantages of external aids

- Using a dictionary is quick and easy, as in *Cheeseman* and *Vaughan*.
- Using Hansard might clarify what Parliament meant. Lord Denning said in *Davis v Johnson* that not to use it would be 'like groping around in the dark without putting the light on'.
- Europe allows background papers to be used so it is sensible for English courts to use them when Acts are based on international rules, as in *Fothergill v Monarch Airlines*.

Disadvantages of external aids

- Using Hansard may not reveal what Parliament as a whole intended. *Pepper v Hart* restricts the courts to considering what ministers said, but Parliament may have decided not to follow the minister's view. Restricting the use to statements by ministers confuses the distinction between executive and legislature.
- Sometimes what the minister said may not be clear. This was the situation in *Deegan (1998)* and the court therefore ruled that Hansard couldn't be used. In another case, Lord Bingham said that if the statement was not clear the courts would be tempted to compare one statement with another and run the risk of questioning proceedings in Parliament, which constitutionally they are not allowed to do.
- There is the danger of treating materials that are not part of the Act as having the same status as the Act and so undermining the authority of Parliament. This is the main objection to using any external aid, though dictionaries are less objectionable than the other aids and are even used when the Literal Rule is applied (e.g. *Cheeseman*).

Rules of language   Revised ☐

- These are common sense rules that have been developed over time.
- The rules of language allow judges to look at other words in the Act in order to make the meaning of words and phrases clear.
- ***Ejusdem generis*** – 'in a list, general words that follow specific words are limited to the same type as the specific ones'. If an Act uses the phrase 'dogs, cats and other animals', the 'other animals' would include other domestic animals, but not wild animals. The rule was applied in *Powell v Kempton Park Racecourse (1899)* in which the court concluded that 'house, office, room or other place for betting' could not include open-air betting on the racecourse itself, because places specified in the list were all indoors.
- ***Expressio unius est exclusio alterius*** – 'express mention of one thing implies the exclusion of another'. If an Act specifically referred to Labrador dogs, it would not include other breeds of dog. An example is *R v Inhabitants of Sedgeley (1831)*, in which an Act referred in a list to coal mines. It could not apply to other types of mines.
- ***Noscitur a sociis*** – 'a word draws meaning from other words around it'. For example, in *Inland Revenue Commissioners v Frere (1965)*, a section of an Act referred to 'interest, annuities or other annual interest'. Because of the reference 'other annual interest', the court decided that the first use of 'interest' must be restricted to annual interest (and therefore not apply to daily or monthly interest).

> **Exam tip**
>
> Read the question carefully to check whether you are being asked to write about the rules of language or one of the rules of interpretation (which are sometimes called the rules of construction).

Tested

1 What are intrinsic aids?
2 Which case illustrates the use of marginal notes?
3 What is an example of an interpretation section?
4 What are extrinsic aids?
5 Give an example of a case in which a dictionary was referred to.
6 Which case confirmed that Hansard could be referred to?
7 Which rule of language does *Powell v Kempton Park Racecourse (1899)* illustrate?
8 What does *'expressio unius est exclusio alterius'* mean?

Answers on p.128

The rules of interpretation

Revised

Over the years, judges have developed different approaches to the problem of interpreting statutes.

They are usually referred to as 'rules', but more accurately they are 'approaches' because judges are not compelled to follow them as they would be if they were rules.

> **Exam tip**
>
> Good answers on any of the rules must refer to case examples. For each of the rules make sure you have cases that you can refer to.

The literal rule

Revised

- The literal rule means giving words their plain, ordinary, dictionary meaning – no matter how unfortunate the consequences. Lord Reid in *Pinner v Everett (1969)* referred to 'the natural and ordinary meaning of that word or phrase in its context'.

- The rule was used in *Whiteley v Chappell*, where the defendant was charged with the offence of impersonating 'any person entitled to vote' at an election. The defendant was acquitted because he impersonated a dead person; applying the literal rule, a dead person is not entitled to vote.

- This rule has also led to unfair or unjust decisions. In *London and North Eastern Railway Co. v Berriman (1946)*, Mrs Berriman was unable to obtain compensation when her husband was killed while carrying out maintenance work oiling points on the railway line. The relevant statute said that a lookout should be provided to warn rail workers of approaching trains when relaying or repairing the track. Giving these words their ordinary, literal meaning they did not apply to Berriman because he was maintaining the track.

> **Typical mistake**
>
> When describing the literal rule avoid saying 'in the literal rule you take the words literally'. You need to explain what 'literally' means.

- It was also used in *R v Porter (2006)* where the defendant downloaded child pornography and was charged under s. 160 of the Criminal Justice Act 1988 of being in possession of indecent photographs of children. However, because he had deleted them and could not access them he was not literally 'in possession of them' and was therefore found not guilty.

Advantages of the literal rule

- The literal rule respects the sovereignty of Parliament. Unelected judges should not change what the elected Parliament has written. Lord Simonds in *Magor and St Mellons v Newport Corporation (1950)* argued that if a problem was found with the wording of an Act, 'the remedy

Exam practice answers and quick quizzes at **www.therevisionbutton.co.uk/myrevisionnotes**

lies in an amending Act'. This is what happened following the decision in *Fisher v Bell (1961)*.

- The rule encourages certainty and people know where they stand. It is better to know that judges are going to take the words literally rather than have the uncertainty of them trying to work out what Parliament may have meant. One result of this might be that people will not waste time and money bringing cases to court.

- Quick decisions can be made. In *Cheeseman*, the word 'passenger' was quickly found in an 1847 dictionary (the year of the statute being interpreted). In *Berriman* it was easy to see that maintaining was not the same as repairing and this would be much quicker than having to work out whether Parliament intended this.

Disadvantages of the literal rule

- It can lead to unfair or absurd results. In *Berriman*, the dead railway worker's widow could not claim because he was maintaining, not repairing the track. This does not seem fair as his job was just as dangerous as that being done by other railway workers who were protected under the Act.

- Nor does it seem fair in *Whitely v Chappell* that someone would be guilty if they cheated by impersonating a live person but not if they impersonated a dead person. The outcome clearly does not reflect Parliament's intention which was to stop all kinds of electoral fraud and it must have seemed a very silly decision to ordinary people.

- It is hard to apply if words have more than one meaning. The literal rule does not allow for a situation where there might be another meaning that is less common but more appropriate (as in *Allen*).

- The literal rule is inflexible and does not allow judges to use common sense. Michael Zander (an academic and critic of this rule) says that it is mechanical and divorced from the realities of the use of language.

- It can result in cases being decided on technicalities, as happened in *Cheeseman* and *Porter*. Both escaped conviction – in Cheeseman's case because the policemen were not passengers and in Porter's case because the images on his computer could no longer be accessed.

> **Exam tip**
>
> The good points about the literal rule are similar to the bad points about the mischief and purposive rules and vice versa. Rigidly following the wording in an Act can produce undesirable results, but it prevents judges doing what should be Parliament's job. Interpreting words in the light of the mischief or purposive rules allows judges to achieve sensible outcomes, but it is not their job to rewrite Statutes.

The golden rule

Revised

- The golden rule is a modification of the literal rule and says that judges should use the literal rule unless it would produce an absurd result.

- Under the **narrow application**, proposed by Lord Reid in *Jones v DPP (1962)*, if a word is ambiguous the judge may choose between possible meanings of the word in order to avoid an absurd outcome. He argued that if a word had more than one meaning, 'then you can choose between those meanings, but beyond this you cannot go'.

- This application was used in *R v Allen (1872)*. S. 57 of the Offences Against the Person Act 1861 made it an offence to marry if you were already married to someone else. The court decided that 'marry' was ambiguous and could have two meanings: to become legally married or to go through a ceremony of marriage. It was clearly absurd to apply the first meaning, as no one could then be convicted of the offence, so Allen was found guilty.

> **Exam tip**
>
> There are two views on how the golden rule should be used – the narrow application and the wider application. For high marks you should try and refer to both.

- The **wider application** is where there is only one meaning but this would lead to an absurd or repugnant situation. In *Adler v George (1964)*, the Official Secrets Act 1920 made it an offence to be found 'in the vicinity of a prohibited place'. The accused was arrested *inside* the prohibited place, but the court held that 'in the vicinity of' could mean 'being in or in the vicinity of' the prohibited place in order to avoid an absurd result.

Advantages of the golden rule

- It allows the court to make sensible decisions. Under the narrow application it can choose the most sensible meaning, as in *R v Allen* and under the wider application it can alter the wording to achieve a sensible outcome, as in *Adler v George*. In both these cases the use of the golden rule prevented an absurd outcome. In *Re Sigsworth (1935)* its use prevented a repugnant outcome (a murderer inheriting from his victim).
- It prevents Parliament from having to pass amending legislation. The court can often make a correction easily by altering just a couple of words, for example, by saying 'on or in the vicinity of', as in *Adler v George*.
- It respects the authority of Parliament because it only allows wording to be altered in very limited situations where the outcome would be absurd or repugnant. In all other cases the literal rule would apply.

Disadvantages of the golden rule

- It only allows judges to change the wording of statutes in very limited circumstances.
- Michael Zander describes it as 'a feeble parachute' because it is not much use.
- It could not be used in cases like *Berriman* because although the situation could be considered unfair it was not absurd or repugnant.
- It is unpredictable and lacks guidelines. Michael Zander describes it as 'an unpredictable safety valve', due to the lack of guidelines as to when it should be used. The Law Commission (1969) argued that the rule was of limited value and noted that the rule provided no clear means to test what the idea of absurdity meant.
- Because the rule does allow judges to change the wording of a statute, it could be argued that it is undemocratic because unelected judges are changing what Parliament has written.

The mischief rule ────────────────────────── Revised ☐

- The mischief rule was laid down in *Heydon's Case (1584)*. Judges should consider four factors when using this rule:
  1. What was the common law before the Act was passed?
  2. What was the mischief that the Act was designed to remedy?
  3. What was the remedy that Parliament was trying to provide?
  4. What was the reason for the remedy?
- Judges should look for the 'mischief' the Act was designed to remedy and interpret the Act in such a way that a remedy is achieved.
- This rule was used in *Smith v Hughes (1960)*, where 'soliciting in the street' in the Street Offences Act 1959 was held to include soliciting

from the window of a house. The court said that the mischief the Act was trying to prevent was people on the street being harassed by prostitutes.

- In *Royal College of Nursing v DHSS (1981)*, the court had to consider the wording of the Abortion Act 1967, which stated that pregnancies had to be terminated by a 'registered medical practitioner'. The House of Lords looked at the mischief that Parliament was aiming to redress – illegal, 'backstreet' abortions – and decided that having nurses (rather than doctors) performing part of the abortion procedure was not unlawful.

Advantages of the mischief rule

- It gives effect to Parliament's intentions. In *Smith v Hughes*, it was clearly Parliament's intention to stop prostitutes from being a nuisance to others, whether they were literally in the street or not.

- It allows judges to use their common sense and save Parliament from having to pass an amending Act. Lord Denning said in *Magor and St Mellons v Newport Corporation* that it allowed judges to 'fill in the gaps' when Parliament had left something out. In *Nothman v London Borough of Barnet (1978)*, he said that judges should use their good sense to do what Parliament would have done if it had had the situation in mind.

- It allows judges to consider social and technological changes. The decision of the House of Lords in *RCN v DHSS*, recognised that medical practice had changed since the passing of the Abortion Act.

- It allows judges to look at external aids like Hansard as in *Pepper v Hart* or international treaties as in *Fothergill v Monarch Airlines*. If the use of these helps judges to see what Parliament intended then it is sensible to use them.

Disadvantages of the mischief rule

- Finding the intention of Parliament can be difficult. Referring to what a minister has said in Parliament, as *Pepper v Hart* allows, may not reflect what Parliament as a whole intended.

- It is reasonable to argue that what Parliament intended can only be seen in what it actually wrote in an Act and that *Smith v Hughes* is wrongly decided because if Parliament had intended the Street Offences Act to apply to prostitutes in houses it would have said so.

- It is undemocratic. It gives too much power to unelected judges. In the *Magor and St Mellons* case, Lord Simonds described its use as 'a naked usurpation of the legislative function under the thin guise of interpretation'. He added that judges were to be guided by Parliament's enactments and not by their intentions. The democratic solution would be for Parliament to pass an amending Act.

- The rule is out of date and does not reflect modern needs. The role of judges has changed as they no longer draft statutes for the monarch as they did in the sixteenth century when *Heydon's Case* was passed.

- It might cause uncertainty if a judge changes the meaning of a statute. In *Stock v Frank Jones (1978)*, Lord Simonds refused to alter the words of a statute because it would have the result that 'ordinary citizens and their advisers hardly know where they stand'.

> **Exam tip**
> Notice that both advantages and disadvantages are illustrated by some examples. You should try and do this in your answers.

The purposive approach

- The purposive approach is used in Europe and Britain's membership of the EU and the Human Rights Act 1998 has increased its use in English courts.
- In *Pepper v Hart* it was made clear that 'the courts now adopt a purposive approach' and can make use of external aids to give effect to the 'true purpose of legislation'.
- The purposive approach requires the court to examine the object of the Act and to construe doubtful passages in accordance with that purpose.
- An example is *Jones v Tower Boot Co. (1997)*, in which the court decided that racial harassment by fellow workers was 'in the course of employment', making the employer liable. Giving the words a meaning other than their natural meaning meant that the purpose of the legislation could be achieved.
- The approach was also used in *R v Registrar General ex parte Smith (1990)*, in which the court decided that although the Adoption Act 1976 allowed people who had been adopted to find out the identity of their natural parents, it was clearly not Parliament's purpose to allow people to obtain this information if they were likely to pose a threat to the parent. Smith had already committed two murders and was mentally ill and posed a risk to his mother, so the court felt that Parliament would have wanted his mother to be protected.

Advantages of the purposive approach

- It makes sense to look at the whole purpose of the Act. In the twenty-first century judges should be able to look at what the Act was designed to do rather than just look for the mischief.
- It gives effect to Parliament's intentions. In the Employers' Liability (Defective Equipment) Act 1969 Parliament clearly intended to protect workers in the workplace and therefore it was reasonable in *Coltman v Bibby Tankers (1987)* to include ships as equipment even though Parliament had not specifically done so.
- It allows judges to use their common sense. Lord Denning said in *Magor and St Mellons v Newport Corporation* that it allowed judges to 'fill in the gaps' when Parliament had left something out.
- It is also sensible to use external aids like Hansard as in *Pepper v Hart* or international treaties as in *Fothergill v Monarch Airlines* if the use of these helps judges to see what Parliament intended.
- It allows judges to consider social and technological changes. The decision of the House of Lords in *RCN v DHSS* recognised that medical practice had changed since the passing of the Abortion Act.

Disadvantages of the purposive approach

- Finding the intention of Parliament can be difficult. Referring to what a minister has said in Parliament, as *Pepper v Hart* allows, may not reflect what Parliament as a whole intended. In *Deegan*, an application to consider Hansard was rejected because what ministers had said was not sufficiently clear.
- It is undemocratic. It gives too much power to unelected judges. In the *Magor and St Mellons* case, Lord Simonds described its use as 'a naked usurpation of the legislative function under the thin guise of

> **Exam tip**
> The advantages and disadvantages of the purposive approach are very similar to those for the mischief rule. But make sure in your answer that you adapt them, so it is clear that you are writing about the purposive approach.

interpretation'. He added that judges were to be guided by Parliament's enactments and not by their intentions. The democratic solution would be for Parliament to pass an amending Act.

● It might cause uncertainty if a judge changes the meaning of a statute. In *Stock v Frank Jones* Lord Simonds refused to alter the words of a statute because it would have the result that 'ordinary citizens and their advisers hardly know where they stand'.

Now test yourself 2

Tested

1 What does 'literally' mean?
2 Why did Mrs Berriman not get compensation?
3 Who said that the literal rule was mechanical and divorced from the realities of the use of language?
4 Which case illustrates the narrow application of the golden rule?
5 Which case illustrates the wider application of the golden rule?
6 What repugnant outcome was prevented in *Re Sigsworth*?
7 In which case was the mischief rule laid down?
8 What was the mischief Parliament was trying to redress in *RCN v DHSS*?
9 Who said that judges should be allowed to 'fill in the gaps'?
10 In which case was it said that 'the courts now adopt a purposive approach'?
11 Name a case that illustrates the purposive approach.
12 In which case was an application to consider Hansard rejected?

Answers on p.128

Check your understanding

1 Indentify the case and the rule the case illustrates.

Facts	Case	Rule
maintaining not repairing		
in the vicinity of		
in the street		
being married shall marry again		
downloaded pornography		
someone entitled to vote		
posed a risk to his mother		
you can refer to Hansard		
a registered medical practitioner		
racial harassment in the course of employment		

Answers on p.128

Exam practice

1 Briefly describe external aids and a rule of language. [10 marks]
2 Describe the golden rule. [10 marks]
3 Discuss the advantages and disadvantages of the golden rule. [10 marks + 2 marks AO3]

Online

Exam summary

- ✔ Remember that internal aids are inside the Act and external aids are things outside the Act.

- ✔ You may be asked about a rule of language – make sure you can explain the rule and can cite a case to illustrate it.

- ✔ In every exam you can expect to be required to describe one or more of the rules of interpretation: literal, golden, mischief and purposive. Make sure you can explain each of these rules and can cite cases to illustrate them.

- ✔ There are a lot of cases to learn in this topic – be sure you can link them with the correct rule.

- ✔ You will have to discuss the advantages and disadvantages of at least one rule and possibly more than one.

- ✔ Remember that the advantages and disadvantages of the mischief and purposive rules are very similar and that they are the opposite to the advantages and disadvantages of the literal rule.

Exam practice answers and quick quizzes at **www.therevisionbutton.co.uk/myrevisionnotes**

4 Judicial precedent

For this topic you need to understand:

- what is meant by the precedent of the courts (*stare decisis*)
- how judicial precedent works: hierarchy, binding and persuasive precedent (in particular the ideas of *ratio decidendi* and *obiter dicta*) and law reporting
- how precedent can be avoided: overruling, distinguishing and disapproving
- the advantages and disadvantages of the doctrine and operation of precedent.

> **Key term**
>
> Precedent is the idea of following what has gone before, so judicial precedent is the idea of following judicial decisions.

Judicial precedent

Revised

- When the facts of a case are similar to a case that has already been decided, the judge must follow that previous decision, especially if it was reached by a higher court.
- This forms the basis of judicial precedent and is known as *stare decisis* – 'stand by the decision'.
- In following precedent, judges are influenced by the hierarchy of the courts and also by whether the precedent is binding or persuasive.

> **Exam tip**
>
> Precedent is based on cases, so it is very important in your answers that you refer to cases.

Hierarchy of the courts

Revised

- In order for the system of judicial precedent to work, there must be rules for judges to follow to make sure there is consistency in the law.
- One way of doing this is to have a hierarchy, so that decisions in the **higher courts bind the lower courts**. Some of the courts are also **bound by their own previous decisions**.
- Decisions made by the **European Court of Justice (ECJ)** are binding on all the courts in the UK in matters of EU law. The ECJ is not bound by its own previous decisions and can overrule them.
- The **Supreme Court** replaced the House of Lords in October 2009 as the most senior English Court. It is bound by the decisions of the ECJ, but as the highest appeal court in England, its decisions bind all the other English courts.
- In 1966 the Lord Chancellor issued a **Practice Statement** which allowed the House of Lords (and now the Supreme Court) to depart from its own earlier decision 'when it appears right to do so'. The House of Lords has used the power sparingly.
- It was first used in *British Railways Board v Herrington (1972)* which overruled *Addie v Dumbreck (1929)* on the duty of care owed to a child trespasser. Also used in *Pepper v Hart (1993)*, which overruled *Davis v Johnson (1979)* that banned the use of Hansard in statutory

interpretation. *Howe (1987)* overruled *Lynch (1975)* and stated that duress was no defence to a murder charge.

- The **Court of Appeal** has two divisions which deal solely with either civil cases or criminal cases. Both divisions are bound by decisions of the Supreme Court and the ECJ, but the decisions of one division do not bind the other.

- The **Court of Appeal (Civil Division)** is bound by its own previous decisions. *Young v Bristol Aeroplane Co. Ltd (1944)* confirmed this, but set out three exceptions:

  1 The previous decision was made *per incuriam*, for example the decision was made without considering a relevant Act of Parliament.

  2 There are two Court of Appeal decisions that conflict.

  3 A later decision of the House of Lords overrules a previous decision in the Court of Appeal.

- **The Court of Appeal (Criminal Division)** is usually bound by its own previous decisions but may take a more flexible approach if the liberty of an individual is involved. In *Simpson (2003)* the Court of Appeal decided that it would overrule an earlier decision to ensure justice for the public at large and maintain confidence in the criminal justice system.

- The **Divisional Courts** and the ordinary **High Court** are all bound by the decisions of the Court of Appeal, the House of Lords and the ECJ. The Family Division and the Chancery Division (Civil Courts) are bound by their own previous decisions.

- There is more flexibility in the Queen's Bench Division when hearing appeals on criminal cases.

- The ordinary High Court is bound by the decisions of the Divisional Courts but not by its own previous decisions.

- The **Crown Court** is bound by the decisions of all the higher courts. Its decisions are not binding precedent, although the decisions of High Court judges sitting in the Crown Court could form persuasive precedent if reported. The court is not bound to follow its own decisions.

- The **Magistrates'** and **County Courts** are bound by the courts above them, but their own decisions do not form binding or persuasive precedent. They are not bound by their own previous decisions.

> **Exam tip**
>
> Notice that the Criminal Division has rather more flexibility in respect of its own previous decisions than the Civil Division.

Ratio decidendi and binding precedent   Revised ☐

- After hearing a case judges present their written judgment. This judgment sets out the facts of the case and the legal principles used to reach the decision.

- The legal principles are known as the ***ratio decidendi*** – 'the reason for deciding' – and are the part of the judgment where the reasons for the decision are set out. This becomes the **binding precedent** for future cases where the facts are sufficiently similar.

- An example of *ratio decidendi* is the rule in *Nedrick (1986)*, confirmed in *Woollin (1997)*, that if a jury considers that the defendant foresaw death or serious injury as a virtual certainty, oblique intention may be inferred.

- Another example is the judgment in *Cunningham (1957)* that to be reckless you have to know there is a risk of an unlawful consequence and decide to take the risk.

Obiter dicta and persuasive precedent

- **Persuasive precedent** is precedent that judges in future cases may choose to follow, but they are not bound to.
- Sometimes the judge may make comments that are not directly related to the reasons for the decision in the case, for example, they may speculate on what the decision might have been if the situation were different. This is known as *obiter dicta* –'other things said'.
- Although this is not part of the case law, it may influence judges in later cases as persuasive precedent. For example, the *obiter* statement in *Howe* that duress was not available to a charge of attempted murder was followed in *Gotts (1992)*.
- Persuasive precedent may also arise from decisions of the lower courts. For example the House of Lords agreed with the reasons that the Court of Appeal gave in the case of *R v R (1991)* when deciding that a man could be found guilty of raping his wife.
- Sometimes higher courts may be persuaded by a **dissenting judgment**, i.e. where a judge has disagreed with the majority. For example the dissenting judgment of Lord Denning in *Candler v Crane Christmas (1951)* was followed by the House of Lords in *Hedley Byrne v Heller (1964)*.
- Decisions of the Judicial Committee of the Privy Council (JCPC) are made as a result of its role as a court of final appeal for some Commonwealth countries (many of the judges in the court are members of the House of Lords and therefore very senior judges). These decisions are not binding on the English courts but they can also form persuasive precedent. For example, the House of Lords chose to follow the Privy Council decision in *Attorney General for Jersey v Holley (2005)* concerning the defence of provocation.
- Sometimes the **decisions of courts in the other Commonwealth countries**, such as Canada, Australia and New Zealand, become persuasive precedent. For instance, in *Caparo v Dickman (1990)*, the House of Lords approved a statement in an Australian case.

> **Exam tip**
>
> A question may ask you to explain what is meant by persuasive precedent. This includes *obiter dicta*, but it would also require you to consider other types of persuasive precedent.

Law reporting

- For the doctrine of judicial precedent to work properly there must be some way in which judges and the lawyers representing the parties can find out if there are binding precedents in existence. This is achieved by an accurate record of law reporting.
- It is only since the development of modern law reporting in 1865 that systematic reporting has allowed the proper development of the system of precedent.
- Even today there is no 'official set' of law reports, nor is there any official selection of the cases to be reported.
- The most authoritative set of reports are those produced by the Incorporated Council of Law Reporting (ICLR). They are known simply

> **Exam tip**
>
> If you are asked to write about law reports make sure you explain why they are needed.

as 'The Law Reports' or the 'Appeal Cases' (AC) and they report cases from the Supreme Court, the Court of Appeal and the Divisional Courts of the High Court.

- A separate volume of *Weekly Law Reports* is also published by the ICLR.

- The *All England Law Reports* published by Butterworths appear weekly and may report cases which do not appear in the ICLR Law Reports.

- There are also specialised reports, such as the Family Law Reports or the Criminal Appeal Reports.

- Many recent cases are now reported on the internet or on CD-ROMs and are often available within hours of the judgments being handed down.

- There are subscription services such as LexisNexis (the oldest of its kind) and Justis, and many case reports are available free.

Exam tip

A question asking for the main features of precedent would require you to briefly describe hierarchy, ratio and law reports.

Now test yourself 1

Tested

1 What is the idea of hierarchy?

2 What does the Practice Statement allow the Supreme Court to do?

3 Which case confirmed that the Court of Appeal is bound by its own earlier decisions?

4 What is *ratio decidendi*?

5 What is the *ratio* in *Cunningham*?

6 What is persuasive precedent?

7 What is *obiter dicta*?

8 In which case was the *obiter* statement in *Howe* followed?

9 Give an example of judges in a case following a dissenting judgment.

10 Give an example of a case decided by the Judicial Committee of the Privy Council that became a precedent.

11 When did systematic law begin to be reported?

12 What are the most authoritative set of reports?

Answers on p.128

How judges avoid following precedent

Revised

Distinguishing

- If there is a case setting a precedent in a particular area of law and the judge finds that the facts of the case are sufficiently different from the case setting the precedent, he or she can distinguish the two cases and avoid following precedent.

- In *Balfour* v *Balfour (1919)*, Mrs Balfour was unable to enforce a maintenance agreement made with her husband. The *ratio decidendi* of the case was that there is no intention to create legal relations when agreements are made within marriage.

- In *Merritt v Merritt (1970)*, however, the defendant husband sought to rely on the Balfour principle to avoid honouring an agreement he had made with his estranged wife. The court distinguished the case on the material difference that the agreement, albeit made within marriage, had been made after the couple had separated.

- Another example is *Wilson (1996)*, which was distinguished from *Brown (1993)*. In *Brown* the defence of consent was not allowed as sadomasochistic acts did not qualify as surgery or tattooing, but in

Wilson, where a man carved his initials into his wife's buttocks with a hot knife, the court distinguished *Brown* and said that this did amount to tattooing.

Overruling

● Judges in the higher courts can overrule the decisions of the lower courts if they consider the legal principles to be wrong.

● As stated previously, the 1966 Practice Statement allows the Supreme Court to depart from its own previous decisions. An example is *Pepper v Hart*, which overruled *Davis v Johnson* on the issue of whether Hansard could be referred to by judges interpreting statutes.

● The Court of Appeal Civil Division has the power to overrule its own earlier decisions, but only in the limited circumstances set out in *Young v Bristol Aeroplane Co. Ltd*. The Criminal Division has rather more freedom. In *Simpson*, it was able to overrule an earlier decision on the basis that justice needed to be achieved for the public at large and that confidence needed to be maintained in the criminal justice system.

Disapproving

● Sometimes a judge may be unable to change a decision (e.g. because the precedent is from a higher court), but feels that the decision is wrong.

● Judges can state that they disapprove the earlier decision and the disapproval may influence decisions in later cases.

Exam tip

You may be asked about the power of either the Supreme Court or the Court of Appeal to avoid precedents. For the Supreme Court the main power is that of overruling and your answer should refer to Practice Statement and give examples of when the House of Lords used it to overrule an earlier House of Lords decision. Distinguishing is more likely to be used by the Court of Appeal and the case examples in the notes are those of the Court of Appeal.

Typical mistake

Students often use reversing as a way that judges can avoid following a precedent. This is not in the specification and is unlikely to be credited.

Advantages and disadvantages of judicial precedent

Revised

Advantages

● **Certainty** allows people to know what the law is, enabling lawyers to predict the likely outcome of a case.

● Because of precedent people can assume that cases with similar facts will be dealt with in a similar manner.

● Without a system of binding precedent people could not be sure that the law would stay the same and that would make planning for the future much more difficult. Lord Reid in *Knuller v DPP (1973)* said 'in the interests of certainty' there had to be a good reason for changing a precedent.

● **Flexibility** arises through the use of overruling, distinguishing and reversing, allowing the law to evolve. Changes in society's attitudes can be taken into account, an example being *R v R* when the House of Lords accepted that a man could be guilty of raping his wife.

● Another example of flexibility is *Malcherek and Steel (1981)*, when the law was adapted to deal with the effect of life-support systems on judging what constitutes the exact point of death.

● Because cases involve **real life situations**, the law develops in a very practical, common sense way. This is better than having Parliament legislate in a theoretical way.

Exam tip

You need to explain why a particular point is an advantage or disadvantage and your answer should also refer to examples or evidence.

Disadvantages

● There are a **large number of reported cases** and this makes it difficult to know all the cases that might be relevant. Judges may only be aware of those precedents that the parties concerned bring to their attention.

- There is also difficulty in determining the *ratio decidendi* of some reported cases because of the way in which the judgment is written.

- Precedent makes the law **rigid** because the strict hierarchy means that judges have to follow binding precedent. Therefore, bad or inappropriate decisions cannot be changed unless they are heard in a higher court that can overrule them.

- The law develops in an **unsystematic** way because judges can only make law on the facts of the case before them. They cannot lay down a comprehensive code to cover all possible situations, as Parliament can.

- It is sometimes not helpful when small changes are made, when what is really needed is reform of the whole area of law. For example *Adomako (1994)* re-introduced gross negligence manslaughter, when really the whole law on involuntary manslaughter needed systematic reform.

- The use of distinguishing creates **illogical distinctions**. There may be only minute and apparently illogical differences between some cases. Too many distinctions of this type can lead to unpredictability.

- Precedent is **undemocratic** because judges are actually making law, which under the doctrine of the separation of powers is not part of their role.

- Unlike legislation, which only applies to events after it has come into effect, case law **applies retrospectively** to events that occurred before the case was brought. This could lead to unfairness if as a result of the case the law is changed, because the parties to the case could not have known what the law was prior to their actions. This is what happened in *R v R*, the effect of which was to turn an act that was lawful at the time it was committed into a serious criminal offence.

> **Exam tip**
>
> Questions may refer to the advantages and disadvantages of the doctrine of judicial precedent. This means the same as the advantages and disadvantages of judicial precedent.

Now test yourself 2

Tested ☐

1 What is distinguishing?
2 Give an example of distinguishing.
3 What is disapproving?
4 Why is certainty an advantage of precedent?
5 Give an example of a case illustrating the fact that the law can change to reflect changes in society.
6 Why does precedent result in the law developing in an unsystematic way?
7 Why can precedent make the law rigid?
8 What does 'applying retrospectively' mean?

Answers on p.128

Check your understanding

1 Choose a case to illustrate each of the following elements of precedent.

Element of precedent	Case
Supreme Court Practice Statement	
Court of Appeal (Civil Division)	
Court of Appeal (Criminal Division)	
Ratio decidendi	
Obiter dicta	
Persuasive from lower court	
Persuasive from dissenting judgment	
Persuasive from Privy Council	
Persuasive from foreign court	
Distinguishing	

2 Complete the tables by adding a comment explaining the advantages and disadvantages of precedent.

Advantages	
Certainty	
Flexibility	
Real life situations	

Disadvantages	
Large number of cases	
Rigid	
Unsystematic	
Illogical distinctions	
Undemocratic	
Retrospective	

Answers on p.128–29

Exam practice

1 Outline what is meant by (a) hierarchy and (b) *ratio decidendi*. **[10 marks]**

2 Outline two ways in which judges can avoid following precedent. **[10 marks]**

3 Briefly discuss the advantages and disadvantages of precedent. **[10 marks + 2 marks AO3]**

Online

Exam summary

✔ You may be asked about the elements of precedent in general or about specific elements.

✔ You must be confident about hierarchy; *ratio decidendi* and binding precedent; *obiter dicta* and persuasive precedent; and law reports.

✔ Make sure you understand about the ways in which judges can avoid following precedent: overruling, distinguishing and disapproving.

✔ You need to know that the Supreme Court can avoid following its own precedents through the Practice

Statement, while the Court of Appeal is limited by the decision in *Young v Bristol Aeroplane Co.*

✔ Look out for a question that refers specifically to the Supreme Court or Court of Appeal.

✔ Remember that referring to cases is important in this topic.

✔ You will be required to discuss the advantages and disadvantages of precedent so prepare at least three of each.

5 The Civil Courts and other forms of dispute resolution

For this topic you need to understand:

- the courts that might hear a civil case and the appeal system
- the various alternative ways that a civil dispute may be dealt with: tribunals, arbitration, conciliation, mediation and negotiation
- the advantages and disadvantages of the Civil Courts and other forms of dispute resolution.

Outline of the Civil Courts

Revised

- The process of resolving a dispute through the Civil Courts is called **litigation**.
- The person bringing the action is called the **claimant** and they sue the **defendant**.
- Cases can start at either the County Court or the High Court, depending on the value of the claim and its complexity.
- A civil claim will be brought in either the **County Court** or the **High Court**.
- There are more than 300 **County Courts** in England and Wales, which handle the majority of civil cases.
- The **High Court** is based in London with branches called District Registries in major cities. The High Court has three divisions: the Queen's Bench Division deals with cases of tort (e.g. negligence) and contract. The others are the Family Division and the Chancery Division.
- Once a claim is started, the court allocates it to the appropriate track.

> **Key terms**
>
> Litigation is the process of resolving a dispute through the Civil Courts.
>
> The claimant is the person who brings a civil action and the defendant is the person the action is brought against.
>
> To sue is to bring a civil action against someone.

Claim tracks and their appeal system

Revised

Small claims

- For actions under £10,000 (up to £1000 for personal injury cases).
- Appeals go to a Circuit Judge and stay in the **County Court**.
- A further appeal to the **Court of Appeal (Civil Division)** is only possible in exceptional cases, for example if the appeal raises an important legal point.

Fast track

- For actions between £10,000 and £25,000 (from £1000 for personal injury cases).
- Appeals go to a High Court Judge in the **High Court**.
- A further appeal to the **Court of Appeal (Civil Division)** is only possible in exceptional cases.

Multi-track

- For actions over £25,000.
- Appeals go to the **Court of Appeal (Civil Division)**.
- From here a further appeal can be made to the Supreme Court if there is a point of law of general public importance.

Other forms of civil dispute resolution

Revised

- There are a number of other ways in which disputes can be resolved.
- Some, like tribunals, are very similar to courts, while others such as mediation are much more informal.
- The AQA specification covers tribunals, arbitration, conciliation, mediation and negotiation. You must be able to describe the main features of each and also be able to discuss their advantages and disadvantages.

Administrative tribunals

Revised

- In order to provide a system for resolving disputes without the trappings of law courts, various governments have introduced, through legislation, a network of **administrative tribunals**. These are designed to provide instant justice cheaply, efficiently and with minimum delay and formality.
- Unlike the Civil Courts, tribunals are specialist and each one hears only cases within its specialist area.
- Tribunals often comprise panels made up of a chairperson (who is usually legally qualified and is now known as a first tier tribunal judge) and two non-legally qualified people who have expertise in the particular field over which the tribunal has jurisdiction. In some tribunals cases may be heard by a judge or member sitting alone.
- Tribunals are now regulated under the Tribunals, Courts and Enforcement Act 2007 which has the following aims:
  - making sure that all tribunals are independent of the government
  - speeding up the delivery of justice
  - making processes easier for the public to understand and more user friendly
  - creating a clearer structure.

Types of administrative tribunals

- Under the 2007 Act there is a **First Tier Tribunal**. This hears new cases and is divided into seven Chambers including:
  - the Social Entitlement Chamber which deals with social security and child support, as well as criminal injuries compensation
  - the Health, Education and Social Care Chamber which deals with mental health and special educational needs and disability
  - the Immigration and Asylum Chamber.
- The 2007 Act also established an **Upper Tribunal** to hear appeals from the First Tier Tribunals – there are four separate chambers including the Administrative Appeals Chamber and the Immigration and Asylum Chamber.
- Appeals are heard by a single judge.
- Further appeals are possible to the Court of Appeal (Civil Division) and, on a point of law of public importance, to the Supreme Court.

Procedure in administrative tribunals

- Cases are decided by a judge and two lay people with relevant expertise (the panel).
- Procedures are more flexible and informal than court and the panel tries to help by asking questions to find out all the information they need.
- They are usually held in private and legal aid is not available.
- All Chambers follow the same procedures and these are designed to make it easier for people to represent themselves.

Employment tribunals

- Employment tribunals hear claims about matters to do with employment, including unfair dismissal, redundancy payments and discrimination.
- Decisions are made by an Employment Judge (usually a solicitor or barrister experienced in employment law with five years' rights of audience) and two lay members (one with employer experience, e.g. human resources manager and one with experience of workers' problems, e.g. trade union representative).
- These tribunals are formal like a court hearing, but are more flexible. Witnesses can be called. Employers are usually represented by a solicitor. Each side pays for their own costs and legal aid is not available. Employment tribunals are open to the public.
- Appeals go to the Employment Appeal Tribunal where they are heard by a Circuit or High Court Judge. An appeal must be on a point of law. A further appeal is available to the Court of Appeal (Civil Division).

Domestic tribunals

- These are 'in house' tribunals set up by professional bodies like the Bar Council, the General Medical Council and the Football Association and are designed to enforce the rules of the organisation.

Now test yourself 1

Tested

1 Which two courts can a civil claim be brought in?
2 What are the three tracks that a case may be allocated to?
3 Where are appeals from the fast track heard?
4 Under which Act are administrative tribunals regulated?
5 Who decides cases in First Tier tribunals?
6 What is the function of Upper tribunals?
7 What is the specialist tribunal that hears claims on employment issues called?
8 What are domestic tribunals?

Answers on p.129

Arbitration

Revised

- Arbitration is where both parties voluntarily agree to an independent third party making a decision in their case.
- The decision is binding and is known as an Award, which can be enforced through the courts.

- The process is governed by the Arbitration Act 1996.
- The arbitrator is usually chosen by the parties and may be a businessperson or lawyer or someone with technical knowledge, such as an engineer or architect, according to the basis of the dispute.
- The date, place and time, the method of arbitration and the powers of the arbitrator are all matters for the parties to decide in consultation with the arbitrator.

Consumer arbitration

- The Office of Fair Trading (OFT) has in recent years encouraged and approved many arbitration schemes set up by trade associations to resolve consumer problems, for example the Association of British Travel Agents (ABTA).
- Usually these involve a **'paper' arbitration**, where the arbitrator makes the decision after reading the documents of the case.

Commercial arbitration

- Many business contracts contain a *Scott v Avery* clause, whereby disputes must first be referred to arbitration. In such cases, it is likely that the arbitrator will be a member or fellow of the Chartered Institute of Arbitrators and as such will have legal knowledge of the matter in dispute.
- Note that the Commercial Court (part of the Queen's Bench Division) can, at the request of both parties, adjourn the court litigation and instead decide the issue by arbitration.

Conciliation

Revised

- Conciliation, like mediation and negotiation, is a genuinely informal way of settling a dispute. It is a voluntary process and the parties will have to agree to the process and to any solution that is proposed.
- The conciliator plays an active part and offers suggestions and advice, which is non-binding but which may lead to a settlement.
- ACAS (Advisory, Conciliation and Arbitration Service) offers a conciliation scheme in industrial disputes. An example was when the Communication Workers' Union (which represents postal workers) and the Royal Mail went to ACAS and strike action was successfully averted.
- The Disability Conciliation Service (DCS) is run by the Disability Rights Commission and it enables disabled people to try to solve disputes (such as no access ramp) with shops, colleges, restaurants, etc. , without going to court, by contacting both parties and offering suggestions on resolution of the dispute.
- The British Vehicle Renting and Leasing Association (BVRLA) is an independent conciliation service which helps to solve disputes between car hire companies and people who hire cars.

Mediation

Revised

- Mediation, like conciliation, is a voluntary process. It involves an independent, neutral third party acting as a go-between to facilitate cooperation and agreement.
- The mediator will often discuss the disputed matter with each party in separate rooms.

- Where the relationship between the parties needs to be preserved, as in family disputes or those involving commercial matters, mediation ensures that the relationship is not soured as it would be by litigation and, should it fail, the parties will have preserved their positions. It also allows the parties to feel in control.
- Commercial mediation is promoted and organised by companies such as International Resolution Europe Ltd and the Centre for Dispute Resolution.
- Mediation in family disputes is available from the National Association of Family Mediation and Conciliation Services.
- Note the importance attached to mediation in the Family Law Act 1996, which aims to take divorce settlements out of the courts and establish family mediation centres throughout the UK.
- Smaller local organisations exist throughout the country, such as West Kent Mediation, which offers a free service run by volunteers to help with disputes involving neighbours in the West Kent area.

Typical mistake

Make sure that you are clear which type of civil dispute resolution you are asked to describe. A common mistake is to muddle them up and talk about the wrong one.

Negotiation

Revised

- This is the most basic and informal of all the civil dispute resolutions and is usually the first method to be used.
- It involves the parties communicating directly with each other to try and reach agreement. The communication may be by any method, for example face to face, on the telephone or by email.
- They may negotiate directly or through their lawyers, who will discuss the case on behalf of their clients and try to reach a compromise. Discussions between solicitors are '**without prejudice**', which means that they cannot be referred to if the case goes to court.
- Low key disputes, for example between a householder and a tradesman such as an electrician or plumber, or between neighbours, are often settled by negotiation, but it is also used to settle disputes between large companies.
- There are no costs involved in negotiation unless lawyers are used.
- There are also private negotiation services. For example, the Bankruptcy Advisory Service takes the side of a bankrupt client and argues their case with the Official Receiver to try to get them a fair deal, such as allowing them to keep their car, for instance.

Now test yourself 2

Tested

1. What is arbitration?
2. Which Act governs arbitration?
3. What are the two main types of arbitration?
4. What is the decision in an arbitration called?
5. What role would be played by a conciliator?
6. Under which type of civil dispute resolution might a third party talk to each party in separate rooms?
7. Which is the most basic and informal type of civil dispute resolution?
8. What does this type of civil dispute resolution involve?

Answers on p.129

Exam practice answers and quick quizzes at **www.therevisionbutton.co.uk/myrevisionnotes**

Advantages and disadvantages of Civil Courts

Revised

Advantages

- It is an advantage that the process is compulsory. Taking someone to court is the only way that you can compel someone to resolve a legal dispute. The other party could decline to lodge a defence or even to appear in court, but in that case, a default judgment would be issued against them.

- Rules of evidence, disclosure and legal argument all ensure a fair process. The **Civil Procedure Rules 1999** introduced timetables and time limits for procedures. This process is supervised by a judge, who is a trained and qualified expert in the law and legal processes.

- The opportunity to appeal is an important benefit of using the courts as it allows someone to challenge a decision they are unhappy with. Appeals from alternative dispute processes are usually not possible at all or only on a very restricted basis.

- Although civil legal aid has been greatly reduced in recent years, it is still more widely available for court litigation than for any alternative.

- Courts have greater powers to enforce their decisions than any other dispute resolution agency. Awards of damages can be enforced by a variety of means, such as sending in the bailiffs or applying for an attachment of earnings order. The courts can also issue injunctions ordering people to cease an activity.

Disadvantages

- Because of the complexity of the Civil Courts procedure, lawyers are usually needed. To employ such legal expertise is expensive. The length of civil proceedings also increases the costs. Even a fairly simple case can cost several thousand pounds and the loser will usually have to pay the winner's legal costs as well. In *Leigh & Baigent v Random House* (2006), the writers of a novel claimed breach of copyright because similar themes appeared in Dan Brown's *The Da Vinci Code*. They lost and had to pay their own legal costs of £800,000 plus Random House's legal costs of £1,100,000.

- The **Civil Procedure Rules 1999** have reduced delays, but the system is still slow, especially if the multi-track is used. Judges have the power to strike out cases where claimants do not meet deadlines, but they do not often do so.

- Unlike tribunals, in most courts judges will not have specialist knowledge of the subject matter in the dispute. The judge will have to rely on the opinions of experts employed by the parties and may not fully understand the technical points being made.

- Many problems result from the adversarial process, which encourages tactical manoeuvring rather than cooperation. It is far simpler, and therefore cheaper, for each side to state precisely what it alleges in the pleadings, disclose all the documents it holds, and give the other side copies of its witness statements.

- Courts are open to the public and the press. This means that private (and possibly, embarrassing details) will be widely reported, as occurred in the divorce action between Sir Paul McCartney and Heather Mills. During that case the judge was very critical of Heather Mills, saying that she exaggerated and made fraudulent claims.

> **Typical mistake**
>
> While most students are able to state the problems of Civil Courts in terms of delay, expense and formality, comparatively few can explain the advantages that these courts have over any other form of dispute resolution.

> **Exam tip**
>
> Exam questions may refer to the advantages/disadvantages of using the Civil Courts to settle disputes or they might refer to the advantages/disadvantages of litigation. Litigation is simply another term for using the Civil Courts.

Advantages and disadvantages of tribunals

Advantages

- Tribunal cases come to be heard quickly and are often dealt with in a day. It is usually possible to specify the exact date and time when a case will be heard, thus minimising time wasting for the parties.

- Tribunals are cheaper than courts. The simpler procedures of tribunals mean that legal representation is unnecessary. Costs are therefore reduced and each party pays their own costs, so there is no risk of the loser having to pay for everything. Legal aid is available at a few tribunals, for example the Mental Health Tribunal.

- The level or formality varies between different tribunals, but as a general rule, wigs are not worn, the strict rules of evidence do not apply and attempts are made to create an unintimidating atmosphere. This is important when individuals are representing themselves. Although tribunals aim to apply principles consistently, they do not operate strict rules of precedent and are therefore able to respond more flexibly than courts.

- Tribunal members have expertise in the relevant subject area. For example, employment tribunals have a Tribunal Judge who will be a solicitor or barrister, usually with experience in employment law, as well as two lay people, one with experience of employee issues such as a trade union representative and the other with experience of employer issues such as a human resources manager. A Mental Health Tribunal has doctors on its panel.

- Without tribunals, ordinary courts would be swamped with cases and delays would be many times worse than they are at present.

> **Exam tip**
>
> Notice that these advantages of tribunals are really ways in which tribunals are better than courts. Remember that unlike arbitration and the more informal types of ADR, tribunals work in a similar way to courts, though with these advantages.

Disadvantages

- The fact that some tribunals are held in private can lead to suspicion about the fairness of their decisions. In June 2012 the UK Government announced a 'Transparency Agenda' which encouraged tribunals and other public bodies to give the public greater access to data and information.

- Full civil legal aid is available for only three tribunals – prison disciplinary, mental health and parole board. Often the ordinary claimant faces an opponent with access to the best representation, for example an employer or a government department, and this places him or her at a serious disadvantage.

- Tribunals are not bound by the rules of judicial precedent and this may result in inconsistent decisions, which creates uncertainty for the parties in a case.

- Tribunals are like courts in that many of them are open to the public and press. Some cases have been widely reported, for instance, in 2008, a case involving the sacking of a Church of England press officer for an alleged affair.

Exam practice answers and quick quizzes at **www.therevisionbutton.co.uk/myrevisionnotes**

Advantages and disadvantages of arbitration

Revised

Advantages

- Parties retain more control over arbitration than over a court case, where the control is effectively exercised by lawyers and the judge. The parties themselves choose the arbitrator, the procedure to be adopted, the time and place and the length of arbitration. They can agree to limit the arbitrator's powers.

- The proceedings are held in private – an important consideration for commercial disputes.

- The parties agree when and where the arbitration will take place and the process is much more informal than in courts. In package holiday disputes, under the terms of the ABTA (Association of British Travel Agents) arbitration scheme, there is no need even for the parties to attend. They send their evidence to the arbitrator who reads the paperwork and sends the parties the decision.

- Arbitration is usually quicker and cheaper than court proceedings. This is because having agreed to resolve the dispute by this process it is in the interest of both parties to set up the arbitration quickly. The ABTA scheme, for example, costs £108 if the claim is up to £2999 which is significantly cheaper and quicker than going to court.

- In addition to having legal knowledge of the issue in dispute, an arbitrator will also be an expert in that area. The Chartered Institute of Arbitrators has around 12,500 global members, allowing the parties to select the most suitable arbitrator for their situation.

Disadvantages

- The arbitrator is unlikely to have the same legal knowledge as a judge and this may result in a decision which ignores important legal points, especially if they are complex and technical. Because the arbitrator is not bound by the rules of judicial precedent, it will be difficult for parties to predict the result and there may well be inconsistent decisions.

- According to s. 68(2) of the Arbitration Act 1996, the parties can only appeal if there was a 'serious irregularity' in the proceedings.

- There may be difficulty in enforcing awards because if the losing party fails to comply, the case would have to be referred to a Civil Court and the court's permission is required (s. 66 of the Arbitration Act 1996). This could be time consuming and expensive because lawyers are likely to be involved.

- There may be an imbalance between parties if only one party has legal representation, for example a consumer against a company.

> **Exam tip**
>
> Look out for questions that do not specify the type of civil dispute resolution you should discuss. For example, a question might refer to 'means other than the Civil Courts' or to 'alternative dispute resolution'. In such questions you can refer to any of the types, but make sure that you identify which type of civil dispute resolution it is and its advantages and disadvantages. Remember that the same advantages/disadvantages apply to negotiation, mediation and conciliation.

Advantages and disadvantages of negotiation, mediation and conciliation

Revised

Advantages

- These methods are likely to be cheaper than using a court or tribunal because it is not usually necessary to use lawyers. Most forms of **negotiation** are free, unless lawyers are used.

However, some private services are expensive, for example the Bankruptcy Advisory Service, which charges £550 for its services. **Mediation** can be very cheap or even free, which makes it accessible to everyone. For example, West Kent Mediation provides free mediation services for disputes involving warring neighbours. Even professional mediators from the Centre for Dispute Resolution will cost much less than going to court. In **conciliation**, the Disability Conciliation Service is funded by the government and provides a free service to help disabled people who have been discriminated against. Anyone whose case is before an employment tribunal has the right to ACAS's free conciliation service.

- The informality and relaxed nature of **negotiation** contrasts with the complex and intimidating experience of being in court. For example, in a neighbour dispute about a boundary, the neighbours can discuss it over the garden fence or on the phone, whichever is most convenient. **Mediation** can take place at a time and place to suit the parties. For example, West Kent Mediation involves mediators visiting disputing neighbours and arranging for them to meet in a neutral location which suits both parties. The British Vehicle Rental and Leasing Association conducts paper **conciliations** which do not involve going to court.

- The problem with courts and tribunals is that they tend to be adversarial, with winners and losers. **Negotiation, mediation and conciliation** are based on compromise so that the parties are less likely to feel embittered by the outcome. The real interests of the parties are also better protected. For example it is much more likely that a trading partner will continue to do business with someone who tries to compromise rather than take them to court.

- All three methods take place in private and outcomes are not publicised in the media, enabling parties to keep business or domestic disputes private.

Disadvantages

- **Negotiation, mediation and conciliation** all work through compromise and agreement, and are not legally binding. There is no authority figure such as a judge to make a decision which both parties have to accept. There is no mechanism for forcing the parties to stick to what they have agreed and this may result in a party being forced to go to court anyway and feeling that they have wasted their time using civil dispute resolution. For example, before they divorced, Paul McCartney and Heather Mills were involved in considerable **negotiation** about the division of their financial assets but eventually this had to be argued in court because neither party could agree. A company could pay for an expensive **mediator** or **conciliator**, reach a compromise with the other party and then find that the other party does not comply with the agreement.

- A judge in court can make a decision based on the merits of the case put forward by each party. However, because these forms of civil dispute resolution are informal and based on compromise it can allow a wealthier party or one that is in a stronger bargaining position to force an unfavourable settlement on the weaker party. For instance, a large and wealthy company may be able to persuade an individual or smaller company to agree to its terms even if they are not really fair to that party.

> **Exam tip**
>
> Preserving relationships is a benefit of these forms of ADR because they are based on compromise and the parties themselves have to agree to the solution. This is different from the situations in tribunals and arbitration. But notice that the corresponding disadvantage is that the decision is not binding. And therefore the process may fail and be seen to be a waste of time.

- Often one party might be unwilling to compromise or feel angry and hostile towards the other party. This makes it very difficult to use **mediation**, **conciliation** or **negotiation**. Disputes between neighbours can often be very bitter – for example an argument between neighbours over a tiny strip of land went to court. Couples who are divorcing can often be very hostile to each other and unwilling to compromise. Union members might be militant or an employer may not be prepared to make concessions, meaning that ACAS **mediation** or **conciliation** will not result in agreement.

Now test yourself 3

Tested

1 Give one advantage of using the courts to resolve a dispute.
2 What does the adversarial process used in Civil Courts encourage?
3 In what ways do the parties retain control over an arbitration?
4 Under what circumstances can a party appeal against an arbitration decision?
5 Give an example of a free mediation service.
6 In what sense do conciliation, mediation and negotiation preserve relationships?
7 Why might there be a lack of equality between the parties in the three forms of civil dispute resolution?
8 Give an example of neighbours becoming entrenched and refusing to compromise.

Answers on p.129

Check your understanding

1 Fill in the table below which gives a summary of the Civil Courts process.

Size of claim	Court/track	Appeals
Up to £1000 personal injury claim		
Up to £10,000 other claims		
£10,000–£25,000		
Over £25,000		

2 Fill in the table below which gives a summary table of the types of civil dispute resolution.

Arbitration characteristics and examples	
Two advantages	1
	2
Two disadvantages	1
	2
Conciliation characteristics and examples	
Mediation characteristics and examples	
Negotiation characteristics and examples	
Two advantages of conciliation/mediation/negotiation	1
	2
Two disadvantages of conciliation/mediation/negotiation	1
	2

Answers on p.129–30

Exam practice

1. Outline the courts (including the appeal courts) which might hear a negligence claim and explain what is meant by negotiation. **[10 marks]**

2. Describe arbitration. **[10 marks]**

3. Discuss the advantages of alternative dispute resolution as a form of dispute resolution. **[10 marks + 2 marks AO3]**

Online

Exam summary

✔ You might be asked which courts (including appeal courts) might hear a civil claim. Refer to tracks as well and decide on the most likely one, based on the information given.

✔ You could be asked about tribunals. They are the most formal of the alternative methods of dispute resolution and their decisions are binding. Remember to refer to examples.

✔ You could also be asked to discuss the advantages/disadvantages of tribunals. Prepare at least three of each.

✔ You might be asked to discuss arbitration. Remember that the arbitrator makes a binding decision and refer to different types of arbitration.

✔ You might also be asked to discuss the advantages/disadvantages of arbitration. Prepare at least three of each.

✔ The other three alternative methods are conciliation, mediation and negotiation. They are informal and non-binding. Make sure you can describe each and give an example of its use.

✔ You may be asked to discuss the advantages/disadvantages of conciliation, mediation or negotiation separately or you may be asked to discuss advantages/disadvantages of alternative methods generally. Notice that these three methods have the same advantages/disadvantages and this material can be used to answer specific or general questions. Prepare three of each.

✔ You might also be asked to discuss advantages/disadvantages of the Civil Courts. Prepare at least three of each.

6 The criminal courts and lay people

For this topic you need to understand:

- the three categories of criminal offence and which courts deal with each
- lay magistrates – their qualification, selection and appointment
- training for lay magistrates and their roles and powers in criminal cases
- the qualification and selection of jurors and their role in criminal cases
- the advantages and disadvantages of using lay people (magistrates and juries) to decide criminal cases.

Criminal courts and the classification of offences

Revised

There are three different classes of criminal offence:

1 **summary** – minor offences that can only be tried by Magistrates' Courts, for example, assault
2 **either way** – offences that may be tried either by magistrates or in a Crown Court before a judge and jury, for example, theft
3 **indictable** – serious offences that can only be tried in a Crown Court before a judge and jury, for example, murder.

Summary offences

- All summary offences are tried by Magistrates' Courts, where the case will be heard by a district judge or three magistrates assisted by a legal adviser.
- There is a right of appeal to the Crown Court against conviction and/ or sentence on a point of law by way of case stated to the Divisional Court (High Court QBD), with a further right of appeal to the Supreme Court with permission if a point of law of general public importance is involved.

Either way offences

- All either way offences start in the Magistrates' Courts. The defendant then has to give an indication of their plea – this is known as plea before venue.
- If the defendant pleads guilty, the defendant will be sentenced and there is an option to send the case to the Crown Court if the magistrates' sentencing powers are insufficient.
- If the defendant pleads not guilty, a decision has to be made about whether the case is heard in the Magistrates' Court or the Crown Court. The magistrates have to decide whether they have jurisdiction (i.e. whether it is the type of case that it would be appropriate for them to try) and then the defendant chooses which court they want to be tried in.
- If the defendant chooses the Crown Court, the case is sent to the Crown Court for trial.

- If both the defendant and the magistrates choose to have the case heard in the Magistrates' Court, it proceeds like a summary offence.
- Appeals will be as for a summary offence if the case is heard by magistrates and as for an indictable offence if the case is heard in the Crown Court.

Indictable offences

- All indictable offences start in the Magistrates' Court with a preliminary hearing.
- The case is then sent to the Crown Court where the defendant enters their plea. If the defendant pleads guilty, the judge sentences them. If the defendant pleads not guilty, the case is adjourned for trial before a jury, with the judge deciding sentence if the jury convict.
- Appeals go to the Court of Appeal (Criminal Division).
- If a person is found guilty, the defendant can appeal against sentence or conviction, provided leave to appeal has been granted.
- The prosecution can also appeal against conviction if the jury has been 'nobbled', i.e. bribed or threatened. Under the Criminal Proceedings and Investigations Act 1996, the Court of Appeal can order a retrial.
- Appeals from the Court of Appeal to the Supreme Court are on issues of law of public importance and leave to appeal is required.

> **Exam tip**
>
> Questions on the courts/offences can be worded in a variety of ways, such as asking you to outline the courts that would hear a particular type of case; outline the types of offence that would be heard in particular courts; or describe the role of magistrates/juries in dealing with an offence. It is important that you look at past papers on the AQA website and make sure that you can answer all the different types of question that have been set.

Magistrates

Revised ☐

Qualifications

- The only qualifications for appointment to the magistracy are that the applicants must be aged between 18 and 65 and under the terms of the Courts Act 2003 they are expected to live or work within or near the local justice area to which they are allocated.
- In recent years a number of younger magistrates have been appointed, including a 21-year-old disc jockey in Horsham and a 19-year-old law student in Pontefract, though the majority are much older.
- Applicants must be able to devote, on average, 26 half days each year to the task, for which only expenses and a small loss of earnings allowance are given.
- Certain people are excluded from the magistracy: police officers, traffic wardens, probation officers and members of their immediate families; members of the armed forces; those with certain criminal convictions and undischarged bankrupts.
- In 1998 six key qualities defining the personal suitability of candidates were outlined:
  - good character
  - understanding and communication
  - social awareness
  - maturity and sound temperament
  - sound judgement
  - commitment and reliability.

Selection and appointment

- Under the Justices of the Peace Act 1997, as amended by the Courts Act 2003, lay magistrates are appointed by the Lord Chancellor on the advice of county local advisory committees.

- Members of these committees, mostly drawn from the magistracy, are appointed by the Lord Chancellor.

- Candidates make a formal application, either in response to an advertisement or by making an enquiry through the government website.

- The advisory committee arranges interviews for shortlisted candidates after their references have been checked. There are two interviews: the first examines the candidate's character; the second, comprising sentencing and trial exercises, assesses the candidate's judgement.

- After the interviews, potential appointees are reviewed by the local advisory committee to ensure that a '**balanced bench**' can be achieved in terms of age, gender, ethnic background and occupation.

- The committee submits its recommendations to the Lord Chancellor, who usually accepts them and makes the appointment. The final stage is the 'swearing-in' of new magistrates by a senior circuit judge.

> **Exam tip**
>
> A question on selection and appointment of magistrates will also require you to say something about the qualifications they need.

Training

- Magistrates' training is organised by the **Judicial Studies Board** and is carried out locally, often by the clerk of the court. It is based on **competencies** – the skills that magistrates need to develop.

- On appointment, all magistrates receive **initial training** – an intensive induction course to familiarise them with court procedures and the theory and practice of sentencing.

- Since 1998, the amount of training has intensified, with the appointment of experienced magistrates as mentors who support the **core training** magistrates receive in the first year and the **consolidation training** they receive at the end of their first year.

- New magistrates are assessed within two years of their appointment to ensure they have acquired the necessary competencies.

- Magistrates who sit in Youth Courts or on Family Court panels receive additional training, as do magistrates who wish to become court chairpersons.

> **Exam tip**
>
> Remember to revise the training of magistrates and take note of whether an exam question requires you to talk about it.

Role of magistrates in criminal cases

- Magistrates have a wide variety of roles in criminal cases and they try 97% of all criminal cases and deal with preliminary matters for the remaining 3%. Their specific roles include the following:

- Hearing applications for bail under the terms of the Bail Act (1976) and legal aid.

- As a panel of three, trying all summary offences and the majority of 'either way' offences; magistrates are advised on points of law by legally qualified legal advisers, but they alone decide the facts, interpret the law and decide whether the defendant is guilty or not.

- Committing all indictable cases and many either way cases for trial in the Crown Court.

- The great majority of defendants plead guilty and sentencing is therefore a very important part of the work of magistrates. The maximum term of imprisonment they can impose is six months for a single offence or twelve months for multiple offences. The maximum fine is £5000. Note that magistrates can send cases to the Crown Court for sentence if they feel that this is appropriate.

- Dealing with requests for arrest warrants.

- Outside the courtroom, magistrates have a private room they go to when making decisions on more complex cases. They also deal with requests for search warrants in private.
- **Appeals** from the Magistrates' Court against conviction or sentence are heard in the Crown Court by a Circuit Judge and two magistrates.
- Magistrates staff the **Youth Court**, which deals with young people aged 10–17. The proceedings are similar to but less formal than those in the adult courts.
- Magistrates concerned in Youth Courts must receive additional training and there must be a mixed-gender bench.
- A parent or guardian must be present at a Youth Court and the youth may be accompanied by a legal representative or social worker. Unlike the adult court, the hearing is held in private and the defendant's name is not disclosed to the public unless it is in the public interest.

> **Exam tip**
>
> Make sure that you are clear what the question requires: a question on magistrates could require you to write about their qualifications, selection and appointment, training or function and roles.

Now test yourself 1

Tested ☐

1 In which court are all summary offences tried?
2 Who decides which court an either way offence is tried in?
3 Where are appeals from indictable offences heard?
4 What qualifications are needed to be a magistrate?
5 Who appoints lay magistrates?
6 How many interviews do applicants have?
7 What criteria are considered for achieving a 'balanced bench'?
8 Who organises the training of magistrates?
9 On what is magistrates' training based?
10 What is the maximum term of imprisonment magistrates can impose?
11 What role do magistrates have in appeals?
12 What rules apply to magistrates sitting in the Youth Court?

Answers on p.130

Juries

Revised ☐

- Juries, although important in our system of criminal justice, are used in less than one per cent of all criminal trials.
- Over 96 per cent of criminal trials are conducted in Magistrates' Courts and approximately 70 per cent of defendants in Crown Courts plead guilty.

Qualifications

- The current qualifications for jury service are detailed in the Juries Act 1974 as amended by the Criminal Justice Act 1988 which provides that potential jury members must be:
  - aged between 18 and 70 years
  - on the electoral register
  - resident in the UK, Channel Islands or Isle of Man for at least five years since the age of 13.
- Some people are either **excluded** or **excused** from jury service on the following grounds:

Disqualification

- Those with a criminal conviction who have received a custodial or community sentence within the last 10 years are **disqualified**.
- Imprisonment for five years or more results in life-time disqualification.
- Offenders on bail are also disqualified.

Ineligibility

- Under the Criminal Justice Act 2003, the only people **ineligible** for jury service are those suffering from a mental illness who are resident in a hospital or have regular treatment by a medical practitioner.

Excusal as of right

- With the exception of those aged between 65 and 70, this category was abolished by the Criminal Justice Act 2003. This change has the effect of enabling clergymen, lawyers, police officers and even judges to become jurors.

Excusal at the court's discretion

- Those with limited understanding of English, students doing public examinations, parents with childcare commitments or problems or people with prior commitments such as booked holidays may be **excused** from jury service.
- However, in such cases it is more likely that jury service will be deferred rather than cancelled.
- Full-time members of the armed forces may be excused if their commanding officer certifies that their absence from duty would be prejudicial to the efficiency of the service.

Selection

- The jury summoning officer arranges for potential jurors' names to be picked at random from the electoral register by the **Central Jury Summoning Bureau**.
- Of those selected (who are not excused or do not have jury service deferred), 20 are chosen randomly by the jury usher for a particular trial.
- These potential jurors – the 'jury in waiting' – are then told the name of the defendant and asked if they know him or her. If they do, they leave the court and return to the jury pool to be used for another trial.
- At court, a final random selection takes place and 12 jurors are selected for a jury.

> **Typical mistake**
>
> Students sometimes confuse jurors with magistrates when describing the selection process.

Jury challenging and vetting

- In the UK, challenging a juror is a rare event, but there are three main ways in which it can occur:
  - Prosecution can use '**Stand by for the Crown**' without giving a reason, although this is only used to remove a 'manifestly unsuitable' juror or to remove a juror in a terrorist/security trial where jury vetting has been authorised.
  - Defence can challenge '**for cause**', which may not include race, religion, political beliefs or occupation. A successful challenge is therefore only likely to occur where the juror is personally known.
  - Both parties may challenge the whole jury panel – '**challenge to the array**' – on the grounds that the summoning officer is biased or has acted improperly. This happens rarely.

- The process of **jury vetting** is conducted by the prosecution with the written permission of the Attorney General and involves checking the list of potential jurors to see if anyone appears 'unsuitable'.
- Vetting is only justifiable in exceptional cases, such as those involving terrorism, the Official Secrets Acts and 'professional' criminals.

Role of the jury in criminal cases

- Juries are used in all criminal cases tried in the Crown Court (i.e. where the defendant pleads not guilty).
- Jurors have to weigh up the evidence and decide what the true facts of the case are. The judge directs them as to what the relevant law is and they must then apply that law to the facts that they have found and thereby reach a verdict.
- There is a partnership between the judge, who acts as 'master of the law', and the jury, who are 'master of the facts'. The jury has sole responsibility for determining guilt.
- In the courtroom the jury listen to the evidence. Notes may be taken and jurors have the opportunity to question witnesses through the judge.
- At the end of the case for the defence and after the closing speeches of counsel, the judge summarises the evidence in the case and directs the jury on relevant legal issues. In complicated cases, the judge also provides a structured set of questions to assist the jury in its deliberations.
- In the private jury room, the jury chooses a foreperson to present its verdict. If the jury has not returned with a unanimous verdict after a minimum period of two hours and ten minutes, the judge may recall it and advise that a majority verdict may be made.
- Since the Criminal Justice Act 1967, majority verdicts are possible (a minimum of ten out of twelve must agree).
- Discussions in the jury room are secret and under the Contempt of Court Act 1981 jurors who reveal information about what went on the jury room risk imprisonment.
- The jury returns to the courtroom and the foreperson announces the verdict.
- The jury have no role in sentencing as this is the job of the judge.

> **Exam tip**
>
> Although juries really only have one function – to decide whether the defendant is guilty or not – you obviously have to say more than this if you are answering a question on the role, function or work of juries. You need to develop your answer by explaining how they fulfil this role, making the kind of points that are in this section.

Advantages and disadvantages of magistrates

Revised

Advantages

- **Cost** Because lay magistrates are volunteers, the system is extremely cost-effective – in 2003–2004, magistrates' expenses amounted to only £15 million. To pay professional judges to deal with all criminal cases would cost at least £100 million per year and switching to Crown Court trials would be even more expensive. In 1998, the average Magistrates' Court case cost £550, compared to £8,600 for the average Crown Court case.
- **Local knowledge** Because magistrates usually live within a reasonable distance of the court, this may provide them with a better-informed picture of local life than judges might have. In *Paul v DPP (1989)*, a case involving 'kerb crawling', the Appeal Court said that the local knowledge of magistrates made it appropriate for them to hear this sort of case.
- **Representative in terms of gender and ethnicity** Almost half of magistrates are female (according to the 2001 Census, 51 per cent of the

population is female) and around 8.5 per cent are appointed from ethnic minorities, which reflects the general population. It should be noted, however, that magistrates are not representative in terms of age or class.

- **Weight of numbers** The simple fact that magistrates usually sit in threes may make a balanced view more likely – in a real sense they sit as a 'mini-jury'.
- **Speed in bringing cases to court** Most defendants who have been arrested will appear before magistrates within 24 hours of arrest for a preliminary hearing. Even those defendants who are summoned to court will be tried within a few months. Crown Court trials often only start about a year after the defendant has been arrested and charged. Following the 2011 riots that occurred in London and other cities, Magistrates' Courts sat overnight and on weekends to provide 'instant justice', which would not have been possible in Crown Courts.

Disadvantages

- **Inconsistency** There is considerable inconsistency in the decision making of different benches. Research has confirmed that some benches are much more likely to impose a custodial sentence than neighbouring benches for similar offences. In 2008 in Lincolnshire, 4 per cent of defendants were sentenced to immediate custody compared to 14 per cent in Humberside and in 2001, 21 per cent of those convicted of driving whilst disqualified in Neath, South Wales, were sent to prison, compared to 77 per cent in mid-north Essex.
- **Biased towards police** Police officers are frequent witnesses and become well known to magistrates. It has been argued that this results in an almost automatic tendency to believe police evidence. In *R v Bingham JJ ex parte Jowitt (1974)*, a speeding case where the only evidence was that of the motorist and a policeman, the chairman of the bench said that where there was direct conflict between the defendant and the police his principle was always to believe the police.
- **Case–hardened** Individual magistrates hear far more cases than individual jurors and this might lead them to become case hardened and cynical about any defences put forward. Conviction rates are certainly much higher than in the Crown Court, though it should also be noted that there are very few successful appeals from the decisions of magistrates.
- **Unrepresentative** Approximately two-thirds of magistrates have professional or managerial backgrounds and only about 4 per cent are aged under 40. The great majority of defendants, by contrast, are young and from lower socio-economic groups, so trial by magistrates is certainly not trial by 'peers'.

> **Exam tip**
>
> A question might refer to advantages/disadvantages of lay people. When answering you should refer to both magistrates and jurors, but make sure that you specify to which of the two the particular point applies because the advantages/disadvantages of each are different.

Advantages and disadvantages of juries

Revised

Advantages

- **Public participation** Juries allow the ordinary citizen to take part in the administration of justice, so verdicts are seen to be those of society rather than of the judicial system. This satisfies the constitutional tradition of judgement by one's peers. Lord Denning described jury service as giving 'ordinary folk their finest lesson in citizenship'.

- **Layman's equity** Because juries have the ultimate right to find defendants innocent or guilty, it is argued that they act as a check on officialdom and protect against unjust or oppressive prosecution by reflecting a community's sense of justice. Examples of this are cases dealing with issues of political and moral controversy, like *Ponting (1985)* and *Kronlid (1996)*. In *Owen (1992)*, the jury showed sympathy by acquitting a father who injured his son's killer despite the strength of the evidence.

- **Better decision making** Most cases come down to essential points of identification or witness credibility. These points are more likely to be decided correctly as a result of discussion between twelve unbiased and legally unqualified people than by a single judge. It is also suggested that, because most jurors sit only once in criminal trials, they are not 'case-hardened' and take their responsibility seriously.

- **Independence** Decisions made by juries have to be made without any outside influence. *Bushell's case (1670)* ensured that even a judge cannot interfere with a jury's decision making. Jury deliberations must be in secret and a breach of this rule could result in imprisonment under the Contempt of Court Act 1981, ensuring that jurors feel free to express their views.

> **Exam tip**
>
> Notice that each of the advantages / disadvantages is developed with examples or further discussion. You should aim to do this in your answer.

Disadvantages

- **Lack of competence** Particular concern has been expressed about the average jury's understanding of complex fraud cases. In 1986, the Roskill Committee concluded that trial by random jury was not a satisfactory way of achieving justice in such cases, since many jurors were 'out of their depth'. Because of inexperience or ignorance jurors may also rely too heavily on what they are told by lawyers at the expense of the real issues. Evidence from New Zealand in 1999 suggested that jurors had serious problems in understanding key legal terms such as 'intention' and 'beyond reasonable doubt'.

- **Jury nobbling** Despite the introduction of majority verdicts in the Criminal Justice Act 1967, it is believed that jury nobbling remains a major weakness. Jury nobbling is an attempt made by means of threats or bribery to 'persuade' a juror to return a 'not-guilty' verdict. In 1982, several Old Bailey trials had to be stopped because of attempted nobbling. A new criminal offence of intimidating or threatening to harm jurors was introduced in the Criminal Procedure and Investigation Act 1996 to try to give additional protection to juries and the Criminal Justice Act 2003 allows a judge to hear a case without a jury if there have been problems with previous nobbling, as happened in the case of *Twomey (2010)*.

- **Cost and efficiency** Jury trials in the Crown Court are more expensive than trials in the Magistrates' Court. The cost of lawyers, judges and other court personnel will be higher and the case will last longer because of the need to sum up the evidence for the jury.

- **May decide unfairly** Jurors do not have to give reasoned verdicts and this, together with the fact that jury deliberations are secret, can lead to the suspicion that some jurors may not decide on the evidence in the case alone. For example, in cases where there is a great deal of media publicity, it has been argued that juries are more likely than judges to be 'swayed' by this publicity. In *Young (1994)* the jury consulted a Ouija board and in 2011 one juror, Theodora Dallas, researched the internet to discover the past criminal record of the defendant.

Now test yourself 2

Tested ☐

1 Which Statutes regulate the qualifications of jurors?
2 Who is ineligible for jury service?
3 Under what circumstances may members of the armed forces be excused from jury service?
4 Who arranges for potential jurors to be chosen?
5 Under what circumstances is vetting of jurors justifiable?
6 What does the jury have sole responsibility for in a Crown Court trial?
7 Which Act introduced majority verdicts?
8 Which case illustrated the value of magistrates having local knowledge?
9 In what respect are magistrates unrepresentative of the community?
10 Name a case that illustrates jury equity.
11 In which case was the trial in the Crown Court by judge alone, without a jury?
12 In which case did the jury consult a Ouija board?

Answers on p.130–131

Check your understanding

1 Complete the table below.

Type of offence	Example of crime	Courts	Appeals
Summary			
Either way			
Indictable			

2 Complete the table below to show the qualifications, selection and training of lay magistrates.

Qualifications	
Selection and appointment	
Training	

3 Complete the tables below by adding some detail and discussion of the advantages and disadvantages of juries.

Advantages of juries	
Public participation	
Layman's equity	
Better decision making	
Independence	

Disadvantages of juries	
Lack of competence	
Jury nobbling	
Cost and efficiency	
May decide unfairly	

Answers on p.131

Exam practice

1 Describe how magistrates qualify and are selected. **[10 marks]**

2 Describe the role of a jury in a Crown Court trial. **[10 marks]**

3 Briefly discuss the disadvantages of using lay persons (lay magistrates and juries) in the criminal justice system. **[10 marks + 2 marks AO3]**

Online

Exam summary

✔ You might be asked about the courts, including the appeal courts that might hear a criminal case. This will depend on whether it is a summary, either way or indictable case. You might also be asked about the role played by magistrates or jurors in such a case.

✔ Questions on magistrates could be on their qualifications, training, selection or appointment, or a combination of these. Make sure you can describe them all.

✔ You could also be asked about the roles of magistrates – notice that unlike jurors, they have a variety of responsibilities.

✔ There could be a question on qualifications or selection of jurors. Remember that they are ordinary people chosen at random.

✔ If asked about the role of jurors describe what they do in the court and the jury room. Remember that their only task is to decide on guilt.

✔ You will be asked about the advantages or disadvantages of lay persons. Remember that they are different for magistrates and jurors. Prepare three advantages/disadvantages for each. If the question is on lay people, you can refer to both magistrates *and* jurors.

7 The legal profession and other sources of advice and funding

For this topic you need to understand:

- the legal professions: barristers, solicitors and legal executives
- the qualifications, diversity and training required for each of the legal professions and the types of work they do
- the background of solicitors and barristers and be able to offer a simple evaluation of this through a comparison of their work and training
- sources of funding: private funding (own resources, insurance and conditional fees) and state funding (community legal service, criminal defence service)
- other sources of legal advice and funding available, distinguishing civil and criminal cases and being able to offer an evaluation of both advice/representation and funding.

Barristers

Revised ☐

Qualifications and training

- Barristers must be graduates, although their degree need not be in law. If it is not, they must take the GDL (Graduate Diploma in Law) or the CPE (Common Professional Examination).
- In order to continue their professional training, potential barristers must become a member of one of the four Inns of Court: Gray's Inn, Lincoln's Inn, Inner Temple or Middle Temple.
- Before being 'called to the Bar' by his or her Inn, the student must be accepted for and complete the Bar Professional Training Course (BPTC) which teaches the practical skills of advocacy and drafting pleadings and negotiation.
- The student must also have 'dined in' on twelve occasions (this rule now includes attending residential courses).
- Having been called to the Bar on passing the BPTC, the student must obtain a one-year pupillage at a set of chambers with an experienced barrister, who acts as a 'pupil master'.
- After the first six months of pupillage, barristers can appear in court in minor cases by themselves. A programme of continuing education is organised by the Bar Council during this period.
- To practise as an independent barrister (as a member of the Bar), the barrister finally has to secure a tenancy in a set of chambers.

Types of work

- Barristers belong to a **'referral profession'**. This means that members of the public usually consult a solicitor first, who will then instruct a barrister if it is considered necessary.
- Barristers may, however, be engaged directly by certain professionals, such as accountants, and since 1996, by members of the public whose cases have been handled by Citizens Advice Bureaux staff.

- In 2004, the Bar Council permitted **Direct Public Access (DPA)**, whereby for the first time any individual or company may go to a barrister directly for advice in civil law matters.

- Under the **'cab-rank' rule** barristers are obliged to accept any case referred to them, provided it lies within their legal expertise, the appropriate fee has been agreed and they are available at the time to accept the brief.

- Most of the work of barristers involves advocacy in any court, as they have full rights of audience in all English courts.

- The other main activity of barristers is as specialists, drafting documents and providing specialist advice to solicitors on behalf of clients. This is known as 'counsel's opinions'.

- Most barristers are self-employed and work in chambers, although approximately 20 per cent are 'employed barristers' and work for an employer in industry, commerce or central or local government.

- Barristers work from a set of chambers with other barristers and share administrative and accommodation expenses. A clerk is employed, whose work involves booking cases and negotiating fees.

- After ten years in practice, barristers may apply to the Lord Chancellor to become a Queen's Counsel or QC, which is called 'taking silk' as they wear a court gown made of silk. Approximately 10 per cent of barristers are QCs.

- QCs are usually specialist barristers in a particular area of law and as such will undertake more challenging cases, especially appeals to the Court of Appeal and the Supreme Court.

> **Exam tip**
>
> In a question on the work of barristers, refer to their advocacy role, but also to their role outside court, for example drafting documents and providing specialist advice.

Solicitors
Revised

Qualifications and training

- Solicitors usually have a university degree, but not necessarily a law degree.

- Any other degree or a non-qualifying law degree must be followed by the Graduate Diploma in Law (GDL) – one-year full-time course, or two years part-time, or the Common Professional Exam (CPE).

- After completing a law degree or GDL, those wanting to become solicitors take the Legal Practice Course (LPC).

- Trainee solicitors must complete a two-year training contract with a firm of solicitors, during which they have to complete a 20-day professional skills course.

- Once these qualifications have been achieved, individuals are entered on to the rolls of the Law Society and are entitled to practise as solicitors.

- After qualifying, solicitors must continue their professional development by attending regular training courses.

- While the majority of solicitors who qualify each year are graduates, it is possible to qualify as a fellow of the Institute of Legal Executives and then pass the LPC – approximately 17 per cent of solicitors qualify this way.

> **Exam tip**
>
> In any question on becoming a solicitor, write a short paragraph on the 'legal executive route'.

Exam practice answers and quick quizzes at **www.therevisionbutton.co.uk/myrevisionnotes**

Types of work

- There are firms of solicitors on every high street and most of their work involves giving legal advice to clients and carrying out non-contentious work, including conveyancing (dealing with the legal requirements of buying and selling property) and probate (drafting wills and acting as executors for the estates of deceased persons).
- Other non-contentious work includes drawing up contracts and setting up companies.
- Solicitors can act as advocates and represent clients in both Magistrates' and County Courts, in which they have 'rights of audience'.
- The opportunity to obtain rights of audience in the higher courts was first made possible by the Courts and Legal Services Act 1990 and extended in the Access to Justice Act 1999. For rights of audience in the higher courts, solicitors have to qualify as **solicitor-advocates**.
- Solicitors as a group actually do more advocacy work than barristers, since 97 per cent of all criminal cases are tried in Magistrates' Courts, where both the prosecuting and the defending lawyer are solicitors.
- Even where a barrister has been instructed to represent a client in a court case, the solicitor still has an important role in doing the preliminary work to prepare the case
- Solicitors usually work in partnerships. There has been a trend in recent years for firms of solicitors to merge into larger partnerships, which in turn has led to increasing specialisation.

> **Exam tip**
>
> In a question on the work of a solicitor, include an explanation of their litigation role when working with a barrister.

Legal executives

Revised

Qualifications and training

- The minimum academic qualification is four GCSEs including English Language.
- Five years' work-based training in a solicitor's office.
- Pass the ILEX Professional Diploma (Level 3) – equivalent to A Level.
- Pass the ILEX Higher Diploma (Level 6) – equivalent to honours degree.

Work of legal executives

- The role of a Legal Executive lawyer is very similar to that of a solicitor as they will have their own clients (with full conduct of cases).
- Legal executives undertake preparation of court cases and provide representation in court where appropriate.
- They are also responsible for general legal work such as property sales, drafting wills, drawing up documents, family law and crime.
- Legal executives may also work for a local authority or private company.

Evaluation of the legal profession

Revised

- Although barristers and solicitors traditionally have different roles, they are increasingly in competition with each other. Solicitors can now become solicitor advocates and take on cases in the Crown Court and High Court; barristers now have more opportunities to deal directly with clients, rather than being referred work by solicitors.

- The main advantage for the public in using barristers and solicitors is that they are legal experts who collectively have experience in all aspects of legal work. In particular, they are uniquely experienced in preparing and conducting court cases and can help litigants present the best possible case.

- Their main disadvantage is the cost, with many solicitors charging several hundred pounds an hour. The dual system of using a solicitor to prepare the case and a barrister to conduct will also further increase costs.

- Increasingly both barristers and solicitors are avoiding the less well-paid work; this means it may be very difficult to find a lawyer prepared to do welfare or low level criminal work.

Background and diversity

- The legal profession has an image of being largely made up of white men and at more senior levels this is still true.

- Both branches are becoming more diverse, however, and women now account for nearly half of all working solicitors and nearly a third of practising barristers.

- In 2008 almost a quarter of people admitted as solicitors and 15 per cent of practising barristers were from ethnic minority backgrounds.

- Of those who were appointed as QCs in 2011, nearly a quarter were women and 10 per cent were from ethnic minorities.

Now test yourself 1   Tested ☐

1   What do trainee solicitors have to complete during their two-year training contract?
2   In which courts do all solicitors have rights of audience?
3   What is conveyancing?
4   What are the four Inns of Court?
5   What are barristers allowed to do during the second six months of pupillage?
6   What is meant by the statement that 'barristers belong to a referral profession'?
7   What is meant by the 'cab-rank' rule?
8   What are 'counsel's opinions'?
9   What proportion of barristers are QCs?
10 What are the minimum academic qualifications required to qualify as a legal executive?
11 What is the main advantage for the public in using barristers or solicitors?
12 What is the main disadvantage for the public in using barristers and solicitors?

Answers on p.132

Sources of advice and representation for civil cases   Revised ☐

- The law can be very confusing for ordinary people and legal services can be expensive. This section investigates where people might find advice and help with a legal problem and explores the various sources of funding that are available.

- The provision of both advice and funding is different in civil cases to that which operates in criminal cases.

Exam tip

Exam questions usually ask either about the provision in civil cases or the provision in criminal cases. It is important that you keep them separate and only refer to the relevant information for the question.

Solicitors

- Usually readily available in all towns and cities and are able to offer professional legal advice to clients on a wide range of civil problems – family law, wills and probate, civil claims, employment, consumer problems, property law and conveyancing.
- In more difficult cases, solicitors will recommend obtaining counsel's opinion from a specialist barrister.
- Solicitors are expensive and will probably charge at least £200–£300 per hour.

Citizens' Advice Bureaux (CAB)

- These are free of charge to the public and are funded by the Community Legal Service (CLS) and local authorities.
- Staff are generally not legally qualified; however, in matters such as housing, welfare benefits and debt counselling, they will have as much experience as many solicitors.

Law Centres

- There are only about 60 Law Centres in England and Wales and, like CAB, they are funded by the CLS and local authorities and the advice they provide is free.
- They employ qualified solicitors and barristers who will advise mainly on housing, employment, welfare and immigration problems.
- Law Centres do not deal with conveyancing or probate.

Private legal insurance

- Private insurance policies will provide legal advice and representation to policy holders, covering most types of legal problem which could result in litigation.
- The most common are motor and house insurance policies which will provide legal advice and representation in the event of litigation arising from a road traffic accident or from an injury arising from a house accident, such as a falling tile which strikes a passer-by. This type of cover will be provided very cheaply as part of the policy.

Trades unions and professional bodies

- Trades unions and professional bodies provide advice and legal representation in any dispute involving employment, such as unfair dismissal, discrimination and redundancy.
- An example of a professional body is the British Medical Association (BMA) which represents doctors.

Other sources of advice

- These include independent advice centres run by charities like Age UK and Shelter and advice services provided by local authorities.

Advantages of sources of advice for civil cases

- Solicitors are widely available and can provide specialist legal advice. They also have access to further specialist help from barristers.
- A solicitor or barrister will be able to provide help with every aspect of a problem, including representation at court.

- CABs and Law Centres are free and often have staff who specialise in housing, welfare or debt problems, which many solicitors will not want to take on.
- Law Centres employ qualified solicitors and barristers and can provide expert legal advice.
- Private legal insurance and membership of a trade union or professional association will provide access to high quality specialist help for every aspect of a qualifying problem.

Disadvantages of sources of advice for civil cases

- Solicitors are expensive and many individual solicitors specialise in a particular aspect of law, meaning that someone with a range of problems may have to consult a number of different lawyers.
- Other sources of advice are also likely to be limited to certain kinds of legal problem.
- Help from trade unions and professional associations is only available to members.

Sources of funding for civil cases

Revised

State funding

- In April 2013 the Legal Aid Agency was set up to administer legal aid and advice (replacing the Legal Services Commission). The Civil Legal Advice scheme (CLA) operates under the Legal Aid Agency umbrella and is responsible for providing advice and help relating to state funding for civil matters.
- The CLA scheme may provide legal help, which covers advice from a solicitor who has a contract with the CLA, help at court or legal representation.
- Eligibility for funding depends on a means test, which considers an applicant's disposable income and capital. Those whose income and capital are below the minimum limits will pay no contributions, but if income or capital is between the lower and upper limits, a contribution must be paid.
- There is also a merits test to ensure that such funding is only given where the case has a good prospect of success and where the award of damages will exceed the costs of the case.
- From April 2013 civil legal aid has been withdrawn from many types of cases and availability in civil cases is now very limited.
- Help provided by CABs, Law Centres and many other organisations is free, but will probably only cover advice and not representation in court.

> **Exam tip**
>
> In an exam question on funding civil cases, you need to make the point that state funding is now very rarely available and that unless a solicitor is willing to take a case under the CFA scheme, it may be very difficult for ordinary people to fund a civil case.

Advantages of state funding

- It provides help for the poorest and most vulnerable people.
- State funding covers a range of services, including representation at court, which is not available from CABs or advice agencies.
- Help is free for the very poorest.

Disadvantages of state funding

- Availability of civil legal aid is very limited and many types of legal problems no longer qualify.
- Eligibility levels mean that only people with very low levels of income or capital qualify for help.
- Where civil legal aid is available, it is still subject to severe means testing, and most people who are eligible are required to make a significant personal contribution.
- A statutory charge may be applied to money or property 'recovered or preserved'. The charge may result in the 'claw-back' of all the claimant's damages, which, as far as the client is concerned, may make the whole action a waste of time.
- When a legally aided client loses a case, it is difficult and often impossible for the opponent to get costs back, as would normally happen in a civil case. This places the legally aided client at an unfair advantage.
- Legal aid costs about £2 billion a year and because there is a cap on how much can be spent, some cases which might otherwise qualify are not funded.

Conditional fee agreement (CFA) scheme

- Under the CFA scheme, solicitors and barristers can agree to take no fee if they lose a case and are able, if they win, to raise their fee up to a maximum of double the usual rate.
- In order to ensure money is available to pay the other side's legal costs if the case is lost, the Law Society has arranged an 'after-the-event' insurance scheme whereby, for a relatively small amount, the claimant's liability for such costs is covered.

> **Exam tip**
>
> A question may ask about a specific type of funding or it may ask about funding in general for civil cases. In practice, the CFA scheme is much more important than state funding and your answer should reflect this.

Advantages of the CFA scheme

- **No cost to the state**, since costs are entirely borne by the solicitor or the client, depending on the outcome of the case.
- Supporters of this scheme argue that, as well as saving public money, the CFA scheme allows the government to fund properly those cases that still need state support and to direct more funds towards suppliers of free legal advice, such as the CAB.
- **Anyone can bring a case for damages.** One of the strongest arguments in favour of the CFA scheme is that it allows cases to be brought by many people who would not have been eligible for legal aid.
- It provides **wider coverage** since it looks likely that the CFA scheme may be allowed for defamation actions and cases brought before tribunals – two major gaps in the existing legal aid scheme.
- The CFA scheme **discourages frivolous or weak cases**. In recent years, apparently trivial cases have been dragged through the courts at public expense, seemingly confirming the view that both solicitors and the Legal Services Commission, which ran civil legal aid until April 2013, were unable to apply the merits test sufficiently rigorously.

Disadvantages of the CFA scheme

- It is an **inadequate substitute for legal aid in uncertain cases**. Most of those who have criticised the CFA scheme accept that in uncertain cases it is a good addition to the state-funded legal aid system, but are concerned that it may not be adequate as a substitute for it.

- **Solicitors may only take on cases they are likely to win**. Critics, including the Bar, the Law Society and the Legal Action Group have expressed strong concerns that certain types of case will lose out under the CFA scheme.

- **Insurance premiums to cover losing are high**. Most concern is expressed about medical negligence cases, which are generally difficult for claimants to win – the success rate is around 17 per cent – compared to 85 per cent for other personal injury actions.

- **Pressure to settle out of court**. The claimant may feel pressured by his or her lawyer to settle out of court (as this guarantees the latter's uplift fee). If this happened, the claimant would potentially receive lower damages than if the case had been pursued in court.

- There may be **conflict of interest between the solicitor and the client**. There is evidence that in some cases lawyers' advice about settlement may be influenced by their need to be paid rather than by the strict merits of any settlement offer.

Private and other sources of funding

- **Private funding** from a solicitor or barrister could be very expensive and in practice is only an option for businesses and wealthy individuals.

- Many solicitors will offer a free half-hour interview and some will even offer their services *pro bono* (free of charge) in particular cases.

Advantages of private and other sources of funding

- For people who are members of trade unions or who have insurance cover, help is available to fund whatever legal services are required as long as the legal problem qualifies under that particular scheme.

- Private funding has the advantage that you can choose the lawyer you want and therefore get the very best specialist help available.

- CABs, Law Centres, charities and local authorities may provide free advice which will not be means tested.

Disadvantages of private and other sources of funding

- With increasing specialisation within larger solicitors' firms, many solicitors will no longer be able to offer advice across such a wide range of issues.

- The help provided by trade unions and insurance companies will be limited to its members and will only cover certain kinds of legal problem.

- Private funding is very expensive and just a few hours' work from a solicitor could cost several thousand pounds.

- Advice agencies like CABs only provide advice and not representation at court.

Typical mistake

Students often write about criminal cases when the question requires them to write about civil cases and vice versa. Make sure you read the question carefully and understand what is required.

Sources of advice, representation and funding for criminal cases — Revised

- State funding in criminal cases is available through the Criminal Defence Service (CDS), which since April 2013 has been part of the Legal Aid Agency. The CDS provides advice and representation, supplied either through private practice solicitors and barristers or through the Public Defender Service (PDS). This is a salaried service, available 24 hours a day to give advice to people in custody and to represent them at court.

- Unlike legal aid in civil cases, state-funded criminal defence continues to be given on a demand-led basis. This means that, although the total legal aid budget is fixed, there is no set limit for criminal legal aid, and all cases that meet the merits and means tests are funded.
- For those who do not qualify for legal aid the only real option is private funding of a solicitor and barrister.
- A person in custody at a police station is entitled to free legal advice or assistance. This can be from their solicitor or from a duty solicitor, or from the PDS.

Duty solicitor scheme

- The duty solicitor scheme was originally created under the Police and Criminal Evidence Act (PACE) 1984 to provide a right to legal advice for suspects detained in police stations.
- It ensures access to a solicitor for advice and assistance is available 24 hours a day, free of charge and without means or merits tests.
- Advice will usually be given by telephone because since 2004, solicitors cannot claim for attending in person unless there are special circumstances.
- At Magistrates' Courts, there is normally a duty solicitor available to give free advice on a defendant's first appearance if he or she does not have his or her own solicitor.

Criminal legal aid

- **Criminal legal aid** covers all types of criminal proceedings and pays for a solicitor to prepare the case and represent a client in court. It also covers the cost of a barrister, particularly if the case is heard in the Crown Court.
- The decision whether to grant legal aid is based on the court deciding whether it is in the interests of justice to grant legal aid:
  - Guidelines are set out in the Legal Aid Act 1988 outlining the kind of issues that the court needs to consider, for example, the defendant risks losing their livelihood; complex legal issues are involved; the defendant has language difficulties.
  - For serious cases such as murder or rape, and in other cases where there is a risk of imprisonment, it will always be in the interests of justice to provide it.
  - For less serious cases, such as minor motoring or non-imprisonable offences, it is less likely that legal aid will be granted.
- As part of the decision to grant legal aid, the court also applies a **means test** and looks into the applicant's financial position and the likely cost of the case:
  - Applicants with the lowest means receive free legal aid, whatever the costs of the case.
  - Applicants with more substantial means will not be granted legal aid if they can afford the likely costs.
  - If the likely costs are large, applicants with reasonable means may be granted legal aid, but the court can require an applicant to pay a contribution towards the cost of the case from both income and capital if he or she appears able to do so.
  - Judges in the Crown Court are able to order convicted defendants to pay some or all of the cost of their representation.

> **Exam tip**
> Notice that state funding plays a much more important part in criminal cases than in civil cases.

> **Exam tip**
> A question on funding in criminal cases should refer to both criminal legal aid and the duty solicitor scheme.

Advantages and disadvantages of advice, representation and funding in criminal cases

Advantages

- The provision of free legal advice to suspects in police stations is an important safeguard and protection for potentially vulnerable people.
- The duty solicitor scheme in Magistrates' Courts ensures that everyone appearing for the first time has access to legal advice and help. Duty solicitors can, for example, apply for bail and advise defendants on whether to plead guilty or not guilty.
- The provision of 'on demand' legal aid ensures that everyone charged with a serious offence has proper representation. Defendants charged with the most serious offences have access to the very best criminal barristers.
- Defence lawyers can fully investigate the evidence and prepare the most effective defence for the defendant.

Disadvantages

- Since the merits test concentrates on the seriousness of the charge and its possible penalty, it is more difficult for defendants to get legal aid for minor offences. Only about half of all defendants receive free legal aid at the Magistrates' Court, and about three out of four at the Crown Court.
- A conviction for a motoring offence or another non-imprisonable offence may still be very serious and may affect a person's livelihood. The 'interests of justice' test means that they will probably not qualify for legal aid, so they may have great difficulty in preparing an effective defence if they decide to represent themselves.
- The only other option for such people is to privately fund their legal representation, which will potentially be very expensive, especially if a barrister as well as a solicitor is used.
- Even if legal aid is granted the defendant may be asked to pay a contribution towards the costs of the case. In practice this may penalise thrifty and responsible defendants who have savings and benefit those who have squandered their resources.

Now test yourself 2

1 Suggest two sources of advice in civil legal cases.
2 What kind of legal problems do CABs and Law Centres specialise in?
3 Which body is responsible for the provision of state funding in civil cases?
4 What is one of the strongest arguments in favour of the CFA scheme?
5 Which body is responsible for administering state funding in criminal cases?
6 What was the duty solicitor scheme drawn up to provide?
7 What is a means test?
8 Besides the means test, what other test is used to decide whether criminal legal aid is granted?

Answers on p.132

Check your understanding

1   Complete the tables below on the legal profession.

Solicitors	
Qualification	
Work	

Barristers	
Qualification	
Work	

2   Complete the table below on advice and funding.

Area of law	Sources of advice	Sources of funding
Civil		
Criminal		

Answers on p.132

Exam practice

1   Describe the work of a solicitor.   [10 marks]

2   Briefly explain where someone injured in an accident could obtain legal advice and representation and how it might be paid for.   [10 marks]

3   Discuss the disadvantages of the various methods of funding civil cases.   [10 marks + 2 marks AO3]

Online

Exam summary

✔ You could be asked a question about the qualifications and training required to become a barrister, solicitor or legal executive.

✔ You could be asked to describe the work of barristers, solicitors and legal executives or asked to compare the work of barristers and solicitors. Refer to the similarities as well as the differences.

✔ You are very likely to be asked about advice, representation and funding. Be clear whether the question is referring to a civil or a criminal case. You need to be prepared to describe the process for either.

✔ You might also be asked to discuss the advantages/disadvantages of the various forms of advice/representation or the different sources of funding. Again, be clear whether the question is about civil or criminal cases and be prepared to discuss either.

✔ Remember that private funding such as the CFA scheme is more likely in civil cases, while state funding is always available for serious criminal cases.

8 The judiciary

For this topic you need to understand:

- the qualifications, selection, training, appointment and dismissal process for each of the types of judge and the composition of the bench
- the work of judges and be able to distinguish their roles in civil and criminal cases
- the composition of the bench
- the independence of the judiciary, how this independence is secured and the separation of powers
- how to make some simple evaluative comments about the selection/dismissal process or about judicial independence.

Selection and appointment of judges
Revised ☐

The Courts and Legal Services Act 1990 laid down the current statutory criteria for the appointment of each level of judge, but these were amended by the Constitutional Reform Act 2005 and the Tribunals, Courts and Enforcement Act 2007.

Statutory criteria

- **District judge**: five years' qualification as a solicitor or barrister.
- **Recorder (part-time judge)**: seven years' qualification as a solicitor or barrister.
- **Circuit judge**: seven years' qualification as a solicitor or barrister or sitting as a Recorder, or three years as a District judge.
- **High Court judge**: seven years' qualification as a solicitor or barrister, or two years as a Circuit judge.
- **Lord Justice of Appeal (Court of Appeal judges)**: seven years' qualification as a solicitor or barrister, but in practice, always appointed from High Court judges.
- **Supreme Court Justice**: fifteen years' qualification as a solicitor or barrister, or at least two years holding high judicial office.

> **Exam tip**
>
> In any question on judicial appointment, you are required to know these different criteria.

Appointment procedures

- The **Judicial Appointments Commission (JAC)** is responsible for the selection of all judicial office holders (all judges and tribunal members).
- It is the responsibility of the JAC to select candidates for judicial office on merit. It does this independently of government, through fair and open competition and by encouraging a wide range of applicants.
- Suitably qualified candidates respond to advertisements placed in newspapers, professional journals or on the Lord Chancellor's

Department (LCD) website and complete an application form and provide a number of personal referees.

- Shortlisted candidates are interviewed by a panel chosen from members of the JAC.

- Successful candidates are nominated by the JAC to the Lord Chancellor for appointment.

- In practice, all appointments of judges to the Court of Appeal are made from the ranks of High Court judges.

- Appointments to the Supreme Court are made under a slightly different procedure because the Supreme Court is a court of the UK, not merely of England and Wales. By convention, two members are from Scotland and one from Northern Ireland.

- The selection panel must comprise the president of the Supreme Court, the deputy president and one member each of the JAC for England and Wales, Scotland and Northern Ireland.

- Supreme Court appointments are recommended to the Queen by the Prime Minister, and under s. 26(3) of the Constitutional Reform Act 2005, the Prime Minister has to accept the name provided by the Lord Chancellor.

- In 2011, Jonathan Sumption QC was appointed a Supreme Court Justice directly from the Bar and with only very limited judicial experience.

Typical mistake

Student answers on the selection of judges often lack precision and are very generalised. Reference should always be made to the Judicial Appointments Commission and to the slightly different process for Supreme Court judges.

Advantages of the selection and appointment process

- It is a benefit of the system that judges have wide experience of the court process before they are appointed.

- If the UK had career judges as in many European countries, newly appointed judges would have little experience of being in court and would arguably be easily manipulated by clever and experienced lawyers.

- The process is now more independent because the JAC rather than politicians make the decision. The JAC appoints through fair and open competition and encourages a wide range of applicants, increasing confidence in the system.

- It is good that there is flexibility to appoint able applicants, like Jonathan Sumption, who have not come through the traditional career pathways.

Disadvantages of the selection and appointment process

- Despite the creation of the independent JAC, it is still the case that the majority of successful applicants to senior judicial appointments are white, male barristers and there has been no significant improvement in judicial diversity.

- In October 2013, there was still only one woman Supreme Court justice out of 12. In the 10 years since the appointment of Lady Hale, 13 new Supreme Court judges had been appointed, none of them women. A fifth of Court of Appeal judges were women but only 18 women High Court judges out of 108. The lack of judges from ethnic minorities is an even greater challenge.

- Because of high earnings made by successful QCs and by senior solicitors, it is certainly the case that many of the best lawyers will not consider applying for a judicial post.

- Despite the additional training now given to judges, it is still possible for a judge to be appointed who will not be experienced or knowledgeable in the specific area of law which they will be involved in hearing. This can be a particular problem with Recorders whose main responsibility lies in trying criminal cases in Crown Courts, but who may be civil law specialists; this same problem can also arise with High Court judges assigned to the Queen's Bench Division.

Training of judges
Revised

- The training of judges is the responsibility of the **Judicial Studies Board**.
- Most judges were formerly either barristers or solicitors and are already highly skilled in legal knowledge and court procedure.
- Most full-time judges will have served as part-time judges, for example as Recorders or deputy High Court judges before their full-time appointment.
- In addition, there is now a Judicial Work Shadowing Scheme which gives eligible legal practitioners who are considering a career in judicial office an insight into the work of a judge. Such practitioners spend up to three days observing the work of judges both in and out of court.
- Trainee Recorders undertake a four-day residential course before sitting in a Crown Court. The course includes lectures, sentencing and summing-up exercises, mock trials and equal treatment training. Before presiding over a Crown Court trial, Recorders in training sit alongside an experienced Circuit judge.
- In recent years, the Judicial Studies Board has received large increases in its operating budget and has arranged more training for judges and magistrates, including courses in ethnic awareness, human rights and computer use.
- The **Civil Procedure Rules** (reforms to the civil justice system) have also prompted further judicial training.
- From April 2011, the responsibility of actually providing judicial training has been given to a new body, the **Judicial College**, which provides initial training for new judicial office holders and those who take on new responsibilities. The Judicial College also provides continuing professional education to develop the skills and knowledge of existing judicial office holders.

> **Exam tip**
> Exam questions often 'link' judicial appointment *and* training.

Now test yourself 1
Tested

1 What are the statutory qualifications needed to be a District judge?
2 What are the qualifications needed to be a Supreme Court judge?
3 Who is responsible for the appointment of all judges?
4 In practice, where are all Court of Appeal judges recruited from?
5 Why are appointments to the Supreme Court slightly different?
6 Who is responsible for the training of judges?
7 How long is the training for trainee Recorders?
8 Who now provides initial training for new judicial office holders and those who take on new responsibilities?

Answers on p.132

The work and role of judges

Work of each type of judge

- **District judges** work in County Courts, where they preside over small claims cases and have administrative responsibilities, and in Magistrates' Courts, where they sit by themselves.

- **Recorders** (part-time judges) and **Circuit judges** work in both Crown Courts and County Courts.

- **High Court judges** are assigned on appointment to a specific division of the High Court. Queen's Bench judges go on circuit to Crown Courts, where they try all serious offences. They may also sit in the Court of Appeal (Criminal Division), together with a Lord Justice of Appeal, usually on appeals against sentencing rather than appeals against conviction.

- **Lords Justices of Appeal** sit in the Court of Appeal, either in the Civil or Criminal Division, usually in a panel of three.

- **Supreme Court Justices** sit in the Supreme Court where they hear final appeals that must involve a point of law of 'general public importance'. Only about 70 cases are heard each year, the majority being tax cases. These judges also sit on the Judicial Committee of the Privy Council to hear cases from the few Commonwealth countries that allow such appeals to the UK.

Role of the judge in a civil case

- In **Civil Courts**, judges may be involved in allocating the particular case to the appropriate track and dealing with pre-trial issues such as discovery of documents and agreeing a timetable to be followed by the parties leading up to the trial itself.

- At the trial, the judge will preside over the court, decide legal issues concerning admissibility of evidence and give a reasoned decision in favour of one of the parties.

- If the defendant is held liable, the judge decides the award of damages or other award such as an injunction.

- Once the case has been decided, the judge will also deal with the costs of the case and decide how much of the successful party's costs the unsuccessful party will have to pay.

- In appeal cases, judges have an important law-making role through the operation of the doctrine of precedent and statutory interpretation.

Typical mistake

The pre-trial work of judges is often omitted from answers.

Role of the judge in a criminal case

- In a **criminal case** tried in the Crown Court, the judge is responsible for all matters of law and has to make sure that the rules of procedure are properly applied.

- The judge may hold a pre-trial hearing to decide issues of bail and the granting of legal aid.

- In the trial itself, the judge ensures that order is maintained and makes sure that both prosecution and defence have the opportunity to fully present their case.

- During the trial the judge will decide any legal issues, such as ruling on the admissibility of evidence.

- Once all the evidence has been heard, the judge summarises the evidence for the jury and directs it on relevant legal rules.
- If the defendant is convicted, the judge decides the sentence to be imposed.

Work of judges outside court

- Senior judges are asked by government ministers to preside over judicial or public inquiries, for example, the Dunblane Inquiry (Lord Cullen), the Hillsborough Football Disaster Inquiry (Lord Justice Taylor) and the inquiry into media phone-hacking by Lord Justice Leveson.

> **Typical mistake**
>
> When answering a question on the work of judges, ensure that there is no confusion between judges trying criminal and civil cases. This is a common problem!

Dismissal and discipline of judges
Revised

- All superior judges – those of High Court rank and above – hold office 'during good behaviour' and may only be dismissed by the monarch following the passing of a substantive critical motion through both Houses of Parliament.
- The only occasion on which this procedure has been invoked was in 1830, when an Irish judge, Sir Jonah Barrington, was dismissed for embezzlement; it has never happened to an English judge.
- It is possible for a judge to be removed on grounds of incapacity through physical or mental ill-health, but this depends on the discretion of the Lord Chancellor.
- When Lord Chief Justice Lord Widgery became seriously ill towards the end of his judicial career, although suffering from a serious degenerative nervous disease, he remained in his job.
- The only example of a High Court judge effectively resigning is that of Mr Justice Harman, who left his position following serious criticism for taking more than 18 months to deliver a reserved judgment in the Court of Appeal.
- Inferior judges such as Circuit judges or District judges may be dismissed by the Lord Chief Justice (LCJ) acting together with the Lord Chancellor for misbehaviour such as a conviction for drink-driving.
- The **Office for Judicial Complaints (OJC)** was set up under the Constitutional Reform Act 2005 to handle complaints about the personal conduct of judges. It provides assistance for the Lord Chancellor and LCJ, who will have to make the final decision.
- On completing its investigation of a complaint made against a judge, the OJC advises the Lord Chancellor and LCJ of its findings. They may then decide what action to take against the judge. They have the power to advise the judge as to his or her future conduct, to warn the judge, to reprimand, or even to dismiss an inferior judge.

> **Exam tip**
>
> When answering questions on disciplining/dismissal of judges make sure you can identify the difference between the procedures for inferior and superior judges.

Evaluation of dismissal process for judges

- The benefits of the system are primarily related to the need for judges to be genuinely independent. For example, it is important that the government should not be able to sack a judge who has made a decision it does not like. The requirement that senior judges can only be dismissed if both Houses of Parliament agree is therefore an important safeguard.

Exam practice answers and quick quizzes at **www.therevisionbutton.co.uk/myrevisionnotes**

- Because judges are free from the fear of dismissal, they can make decisions they feel to be just, even if such decisions are unpopular; this increases public confidence in using the courts.

- It is sensible that there is a means of removing judges in extreme cases, and although instances of the dismissal of inferior judges are rare, the fact that this is ultimately possible is important. It is also helpful that judges have to retire at 70, as this reduces the risks of problems caused by age-related degeneracy.

- On the other hand, the examples of Mr Justice Harman and Lord Widgery show that the system makes it very difficult to remove a senior judge who is incompetent or whose behaviour is inappropriate. It is of concern that it is virtually impossible to sack judges of High Court rank or above, whatever they do or say.

Judicial independence

Revised

- In the UK's legal system, great importance is attached to the idea that judges should be independent from any pressure from the government in particular, and from any political or other pressure groups, so that those who appear before them and the wider public can have confidence that their cases will be decided fairly and in accordance with the law.

- Judge must be free of any improper influence which could come from the Government or Parliament or from the media and pressure groups as well as from the parties in a case.

- This theory of judicial independence owes its origin to French philosopher **Montesquieu** with his theory of the **'separation of powers'**. In this, he argued that the only way to safeguard individual liberties is to ensure that the power of the state is divided between three separate and independent arms: the legislature, the executive and the judiciary. Each arm should operate independently and be checked and balanced by the other two.

How judicial independence is secured
Tenure of office

- In England, all superior judges hold office 'during good behaviour', subject to removal only by the monarch by means of an address presented by both Houses of Parliament (Act of Settlement 1701). This has never happened to an English judge.

- Under the Constitutional Reform Act 2005, the OJC was appointed to investigate complaints made against judges.

Judicial immunity from suit

- No judge may be sued in respect of anything done while acting in his or her judicial capacity.

Immunity from parliamentary criticism

- No criticism of an individual judge may be made in either House except by way of a substantive motion.

- Political neutrality is also preserved in that judicial salaries are charged upon the consolidated fund, which removes the opportunity for an annual debate.

Evaluation of judicial independence

- The value of judicial independence is highlighted by the increase in judicial review cases, in which judges are required to examine the legality or procedural correctness of government decisions.
- The responsibility of the judiciary to protect citizens against unlawful acts of government has thus increased, and with it the need for the judiciary to be independent of government.
- There have been many instances where judges have overruled the decisions of government ministers, for example *A v Home Secretary (2004)*, when the House of Lords ruled that control orders were unlawful.
- In recent years, there have been many judicial decisions concerning immigration appeals and appeals against deportation orders where Home Secretaries' decisions have been successfully challenged.
- The independence of the judiciary is particularly necessary when judges have to chair inquiries into major cases and national events, for example the Hillsborough disaster, the Stephen Lawrence murder, the Arms-to-Iraq controversy and the Leveson Inquiry into the conduct of the press, including allegations of phone-hacking.

Now test yourself 2

Tested ☐

1 Which judges try all serious criminal offences?
2 Approximately how many cases are heard by the Supreme Court each year?
3 What decisions does a judge have to make at the end of a civil case?
4 Once all the evidence has been heard in a criminal case, what does the judge need to do next?
5 How can superior judges be dismissed?
6 How can inferior judges be dismissed?
7 Which body hears complaints about the personal conduct of judges?
8 What is the origin of the theory of judicial independence?
9 What are the three ways in which judicial independence is secured?
10 What has highlighted the importance of judicial independence?

Answers on p.132–133

Check your understanding

1 Complete the table below on the role of judges.

Role of judges in civil cases	
Role of judges in criminal cases	

2 Complete the table below on judicial independence

Meaning	
How secured	1
	2
	3
Evaluation	1
	2
	3

Answers on p.133

Exam practice answers and quick quizzes at **www.therevisionbutton.co.uk/myrevisionnotes**

Exam practice

1 Briefly describe how both superior and inferior judges are selected and appointed. [10 marks]

2 Describe the work of a judge in a Crown Court trial. [10 marks]

3 Discuss the importance of judicial independence. [10 marks plus 2 for AO3]

Online

Exam summary

✔ You could be asked to describe how judges are chosen or asked to discuss the advantages/disadvantages of the selection process. Refer to the role now played by the JAC and to the fact that the appointment process is more independent than it used to be.

✔ You may be asked to describe the process for dismissing judges and perhaps to discuss the advantages/disadvantages of the fact that it is so difficult to dismiss a judge. Remember that this helps to ensure the independence of judges, but it might result in bad judges staying in office.

✔ You could be asked to describe the work of a judge in a criminal or civil case. Be clear which is being asked and prepare for a question on either.

✔ You could also be asked to describe how the independence of judges is secured and discuss why judicial independence is important. Notice that this raises similar points to a question on dismissal of judges. Refer to the idea of the separation of powers.

Introduction to Unit 2: The concept of liability

Unit 2 covers substantive law and introduces you to criminal law and an area of civil law. It is divided into the following:

Section A: Introduction to criminal liability

9 Underlying principles of criminal liability including non-fatal offences
10 The courts: procedure and sentencing

Section B: Introduction to tort

11 Liability in negligence
12 The courts: procedures and damages

Section C: Introduction to contract

13 Formation of contract
14 Breach of contract and the courts: procedure and damages

The Unit 2 exam

- The exam lasts 1 hour 30 minutes and you are required to answer questions on Section A and either Section B or Section C.
- Each section has six questions; two are theoretical questions and the other four are based on a scenario.
- You must answer all the questions in the two sections you choose.
- Although the total marks for each question are the same (45 marks plus 2 marks for AO3), the marks for individual questions in each section vary and can be worth between 5 and 10 marks.

Help from the exam board

- As with Unit 1, AQA provide guidance in the specification on what you have to cover in each section.
- The AQA website also has past papers, mark schemes and examiner reports.

Preparing for the exam

- Theoretical questions require knowledge and understanding of the relevant rules and principles.

- Questions based on a scenario also require knowledge and understanding, but they also require application to the facts in the scenario.

- As with Unit 1, it is important to look at the material provided by the exam board. In particular it is very important to look at the range of past exam questions, so that you can see what kind of questions are asked in each of the sections.

- You should also look at the mark schemes and examiner reports to be confident that you are properly prepared.

- To achieve high marks answers need to provide information which is relevant to the question being asked. The level of detail needed will depend on the question. For example, a two-part question will expect less detail on each part than a whole question on just one aspect.

- Answers which are thin and generalised will not achieve high marks. Learn the material thoroughly, so that you go into the exam with the appropriate knowledge.

- You also need to understand what you are learning, so that you can adapt it to answer questions that are slightly different to those that you may have answered before.

- You will be given a scenario that you have not seen before and you will need to read it carefully before you answer the questions. Application questions require you to comment on how the relevant rules apply to the specific facts in the scenario.

- Spending the right amount of time on each question is important. Because the questions are worth different marks you will need to spend longer on the higher mark questions than the lower mark questions.

- Practice in answering questions under exam conditions is very important. You need to be confident that you can write appropriate answers to each of the questions in the time allowed.

Use of authorities

- In many Unit 2 answers you will need to refer to authorities – cases or Acts of Parliament.

- When using cases you will not need to refer to the date of the case and with complicated case names it is sufficient to use a shortened simplified version – examiners will know which case you mean. Criminal cases are usually written *R v*, but in most AS Law textbooks (and this Revision Guide) cases are referred to just by the name of the defendant (e.g. *Cunningham, Miller*).

- When referring to an Act of Parliament, you must include the date of the Act as well.

9 Underlying principles of criminal liability including non-fatal offences

For this topic you need to understand:

- *actus reus*, including omissions and causation
- *mens rea* – meaning intention or recklessness
- transferred malice
- coincidence of *actus reus* and *mens rea*
- srict liability
- non-fatal offences (i.e. offences against the person that do not result in death)
- offences that must be studied: assault, battery (known together as common assault), the three offences under the Offences Against the Person Act 1861: actual bodily harm (s. 47), wounding/grievous bodily harm (s. 20) and wounding/grievous bodily harm with intent (s. 18).

> **Exam tip**
>
> The first questions in the Unit 2 exam will be general explanatory questions which are not based on an actual scenario. Do not, therefore, refer to any of the specific issues raised in the scenario.

Actus reus — Revised ☐

- *Actus reus* means the unlawful act – the physical act.
- It must be a **voluntary** act, i.e. it must be an act of will in which the mind is in control of the body and not a situation like a fit or a reflex action as in *Hill v Baxter (1958)* where the example was used of a driver attacked by a swarm of bees.
- In 'result crimes' it is the act plus the consequence. These are crimes where the defendant's actions cause the prohibited result. For example, in murder it is doing something which leads to the consequence of death and in ABH the result must be actual bodily harm. The act must be both the factual cause and the legal cause.
- It could also be a state of affairs, for example, someone is in possession of drugs. The *actus reus* of the offence is in the condition or circumstances rather than in any action. In *Larsonneur (1933)*, the defendant was illegally in the UK and in *Winzar (1983)* the defendant was in a drunken state on the highway.
- An **omission** (a failure to act) cannot usually form the *actus reus*, but there are exceptions where the law imposes a duty to act, as for example in *Pittwood (1902)* and in *Miller (1983)*.

> **Key terms**
>
> *Actus reus* means the physical act which is the basis for the crime.
>
> A voluntary act is one in which the mind is in control of the body.

> **Exam tip**
>
> You need only refer briefly to omissions when answering a question on *actus reus*. Sometimes a whole question is asked on omissions, which is why there is a separate, more detailed section on this later.

Omissions — Revised ☐

- The general rule is that the *actus reus* must involve an act and that you cannot be guilty of a criminal offence by a failure to act.
- There are, however, circumstances in which an omission can form the *actus reus*, for example where you have a contractual duty and fail to act. In *Pittwood* a railway crossing gatekeeper failed to shut the gate and a person was killed by a train.
- People like police officers have a duty to act because of their official position. In *Dytham (1979)* a policeman did nothing when someone was being attacked.

- Sometimes a statute may create an offence based on omission, for example it is an offence not to wear a crash helmet on a motorbike or a seatbelt in a car.

- A duty can also arise because of a relationship, for example a parent has a duty to care for their child and a failure to feed them would be a criminal offence.

- A duty to care for someone voluntarily will also create a duty to act. An example is *Stone and Dobinson (1977)*, where a couple did nothing to help an anorexic sister whom they had invited to live with them and who was neglecting herself and eventually died.

- People also have a duty to put right a dangerous situation they have created. In *Miller* a man in a hostel fell asleep while smoking and set fire to his bed. But when he realised what he had done he did nothing to put the situation right and it was this failure to act, rather than his original conduct, that made him liable.

Exam tip

If you are asked to explain what is meant by *actus reus* in a general question, focus on the rule that the act must be voluntary and then consider the various common law rules on omissions.

Causation

- In 'result crimes' a causal link must be proved between the defendant's actions and the consequence.

Factual causation

- This is where something is a cause of some kind so that 'but for' the thing happening the consequence would not have occurred.

- It must be more than a tiny or trivial cause. In *White (1910)*, where the defendant tried to poison his mother, he was not even a factual cause because his mother died of a heart attack before the poison could take effect.

Legal causation

- This is where a cause is the substantial and operating cause (*Smith*) or a significant cause (*Cheshire*).

- For any event there might be a number of factual causes, but only a 'significant' or 'operating and substantial' cause will be important enough to be considered a legal cause. In *Smith (1959)* the victim, who had been stabbed in a fight between soldiers, received 'thoroughly bad' treatment, but clearly died from loss of blood caused by the stab wound, so Smith was the operating and substantial cause.

- In *Cheshire (1991)* the victim had been shot, but died as a result of rare complications caused by a breathing tube inserted by doctors. Cheshire was still a significant cause, however, because the treatment was for injuries caused by him.

- **Intervening acts** will only break the chain of causation if they are unforeseeable. For example, in the case of *Pagett (1983)* where the defendant used a girl as a shield and opened fire on the police, the chain was not broken because it was foreseeable that the police would fire back.

- In **medical cases** if the original wound is still the operating and substantial cause, then any actions by doctors, even if negligent, will not break the chain of causation and the original wound will still be the cause of death. But if the original wound is simply the setting in which another cause operates, the chain of causation will be broken. This happened in *Jordan (1956)* where the victim made a good

Exam tip

In answering a 'general explanatory' question on causation, the main part of the answer must focus on the various legal rules on causation – the 'but for' factual rule needs a simple explanation of the rule with a brief summary of the facts in *White* (or *Pagett*). If the causation question also requires some consideration of the scenario, consider which legal rules are actually relevant and explain these fully.

recovery, but during recuperation was given a drug to which he was allergic and doctors confirmed that his death was not caused by the original wound.

- In 'escape cases' the chain of causation will not be broken as long as the victim's actions are foreseeable. For example, in *Roberts (1971)* the chain was not broken because it was foreseeable that the victim may jump out of a moving car to escape unwanted sexual advances. However, in *Williams (1992)* the chain was broken because it was not foreseeable that the hitchhiker would jump out of the moving car when the driver tried to steal his wallet.

- Sometimes a pre-existing weakness or medical condition makes the consequence more serious for the victim than it would have been for other people. The '**thin skull rule**' means that you must take your victim as you find him and are therefore liable for all the consequences. The rule covers physical and mental conditions and even the victim's beliefs and values as in *Blaue (1975)*, where the victim refused to have a blood transfusion because of her religious beliefs and died as a consequence.

Key terms

Factual causation means a cause of some kind and 'but for' this event occurring the consequence would not have happened. Legal causation means that the cause is an important one – an 'operating and substantial' or 'significant' cause.

Now test yourself 1

Tested

1. What is a voluntary act?
2. Give a case example of a voluntary act.
3. Explain what a state of affairs is.
4. Give one example of a state of affairs.
5. What is an omission?
6. Explain the usual rule on omissions and *actus reus*.
7. Give two exceptions to the usual rule on omissions and *actus reus*.
8. Why was the administration of poison by *White* not a factual cause of his mother's death?
9. What rule do the cases of *Smith* and *Cheshire* illustrate?
10. Why did the actions of the police in *Pagett* not break the chain of causation?
11. Give an example of an 'escape case'.
12. Explain what the thin skull rule is.

Answers on p.133

Mens rea

Revised

- This is the mental element in the crime – the state of mind – which is necessary for the crime in question. There are a number of different states of mind that can amount to *mens rea*.

Intent

- **Intention** is where you act deliberately or you make something your aim and purpose. In *Mohan (1975)* it was defined as a decision to bring about a consequence.

- **Oblique intent** is where the defendant claims to have some other purpose, for example in *Hancock and Shankland (1986)* they claimed that they wanted to stop the miner getting to work. The *Nedrick* rule (confirmed in *Woollin*) applies in these cases. If the defendant knew that death or serious injury was virtually certain as a result of his actions and yet went ahead, the jury can conclude that the result was intended.

Exam tip

In a general question on explaining the meaning of *mens rea*, make sure you have learnt the meaning of oblique intent – without this, your answer cannot be 'sound'.

- In *Woollin (1998)* the defendant lost his temper and threw a baby towards his pram. The baby hit the wall and suffered head injuries from which he died.
- In *Matthews and Alleyne (2003)* the defendants threw their victim into the Thames where he drowned. They knew that death or serious injury was virtually certain as they knew their victim could not swim.

Recklessness

Recklessness is where someone knows there is a risk and continues with the act.

The case of *R v G and Others (2003)* confirms that the principle of recklessness is that set out in *Cunningham (1957)* which is that the defendant appreciated that their actions created an unjustified risk and went ahead with the action anyway.

Transferred malice

- **Transferred malice** is where a person injures someone other than their intended victim.
- The rule is that the malice (intention) is transferred from the intended to the actual victim as long as the crime is the same as the one the person would have been charged with in respect of the intended victim.
- An example is *Latimer (1886)* where a man aimed to hit another man with a belt, but hit a woman by mistake. The malice was transferred from the intended victim to the woman.
- The malice cannot be transferred between different crimes. An example is *Pembliton (1874)*, in which the defendant threw a stone at the intended victim but smashed a window instead. The crime was different, so transferred malice did not apply.

> **Typical mistake**
>
> Students often confuse oblique intent with recklessness.

> **Key terms**
>
> *Mens rea* means the guilty mind – the mental element in a crime.
>
> Intention is where you act deliberately or make something your aim and purpose.
>
> Oblique intent is where you know something is a virtually certain consequence of your action and yet you continue with the action.
>
> Recklessness is where you know there is a risk of a consequence and yet you continue with the action.

> **Exam tip**
>
> You could be asked to apply transferred malice to a scenario.

Coincidence of *mens rea* and *actus reus*   Revised ☐

- The rule is that *actus reus* and *mens rea* usually have to be present at the same time. For example if someone drives to someone's house intending to kill them, but accidentally runs them over on the way and they die, this is not murder because at the time of the killing (*actus reus*) there was no *mens rea*.
- However, in situations where there is really a series of acts and *mens rea* was present at some stage, the law says that the *mens rea* applies to the whole series.
- For example in *Thabo Meli (1954)* the defendants beat a man up and thought he was dead. So they threw him over a cliff and he later died of exposure. Their claim that they had no *mens rea* at the time when they threw him over the cliff because they thought he was already dead was rejected and the court decided that because they had *mens rea* when they attacked him, the *mens rea* applied to the whole series of acts.
- Another example is *Fagan (1969)*. The defendant was asked by a policeman to move his car. He moved it by mistake onto the policeman's foot, but then he deliberately left it there. The offence he was charged with (battery) involves an act, and in this case when he did the act (driving onto the foot) he had no *mens rea*. Again, the court decided that there was one continuous act and he certainly had *mens rea* when he refused to move the car.

> **Exam tip**
>
> In an exam question on coincidence, you should explain both *Thabo Meli* and *Fagan* – in the former, there was continuing *mens rea*; in the latter, continuing *actus reus*.

Strict liability

- Strict liability offences are ones that do not require any *mens rea*. Guilt is determined purely on the basis of *actus reus*.

- Almost all strict liability offences are **statutory**, i.e. they are defined in Acts of Parliament. They are also **regulatory** in nature. These types of offences are designed to protect the public and are not thought of as being truly criminal in nature.

- Many strict liability offences concern road traffic or health and safety. In *Callow v Tillstone (1900)* a butcher was convicted of selling contaminated meat even though he asked a vet to examine the meat and he was assured by the vet that it was fit for human consumption. In *Harrow LBC v Shah (1999)* a shop owner was prosecuted for selling lottery tickets to a person under 16, even though he took reasonable precautions to prevent this. In *Alphacell v Woodward (1972)* the offence was causing polluted matter to enter a river.

- There is a presumption of *mens rea* if the offence is 'truly criminal', i.e. where the crime is one that will carry the stigma of being the kind of offence people would think of as criminal as opposed to a technical offence and where the penalty could involve imprisonment. For example in *Sweet v Parsley (1970)*, the defendant's conviction was for being concerned in the management of premises that were being used for the smoking of cannabis. The court decided that real social stigma attached to this offence and therefore *mens rea* was needed.

> **Typical mistake**
>
> Students often refer to absolute liability offences as if they were the same as strict liability. They are not.

> **Exam tip**
>
> In an answer, ensure that cases are correctly explained, especially *Sweet v Parsley*.

Advantages of strict liability offences

- Strict liability offences help protect society by promoting greater care over matters of public safety.

- They are easier to enforce as there is no need to prove *mens rea*.

- They save court time as people are more likely to plead guilty.

Disadvantages of strict liability offences

- Makes people guilty who are not blameworthy.

- Even these who have taken all possible care will be found guilty and can be punished – as happened in *Shah*.

Now test yourself 2

1 Explain what is meant by intention.
2 Explain what is meant by oblique intent.
3 Which case is a good illustration of the oblique intent rule?
4 Explain what is meant by recklessness.
5 What are the two cases that confirm the definition of recklessness?
6 Which rule does the case of *Latimer* illustrate?
7 What principle is illustrated in *Thabo Meli* and *Fagan*?
8 What are strict liability offences?
9 Give a case example of strict liability.
10 In what kind of cases is there a presumption of *mens rea*?
11 Suggest an advantage of strict liability.
12 Suggest a disadvantage of strict liability.

Answers on p.133–134

Non-fatal offences

Revised ☐

- There are five non-fatal offences that have to be studied.

- Assault and battery are common law offences. They are not defined in any Act, although the Criminal Justice Act 1988 states the maximum sentences for each and establishes that they are summary offences. Together they are referred to as common assault.

- The remaining three offences are all defined in the Offences Against the Person Act 1861 – s. 47 actual bodily harm, s. 20 wounding or inflicting grievous bodily harm and s. 18 wounding or causing grievous bodily harm with intent.'

> **Typical mistake**
>
> To state that the *actus reus* means that the victim was afraid – there is no such requirement.

Assault

Revised ☐

- The *actus reus* is any act which makes the victim apprehend the immediate infliction of unlawful force. In *Smith v Woking Police (1983)* it was looking at a woman in her nightclothes through a window. In *Logdon (1976)* a man showed his victim a gun in a drawer. The victim did not realise that this was a replica and became terrified.

- Words alone can be enough and even a silent phone call, as in *Ireland (1998)*. In *Constanza (1997)* letters sent by a stalker were interpreted as clear threats and there was 'fear of violence at some time not excluding the immediate future'.

- Words can also annul assault – this means that words can make it clear that violence is not going to be used. In *Turberville v Savage (1669)* the words 'if it were not Assize time I would run you through with my sword' annulled the assault.

- The *mens rea* is an intention to cause the victim to apprehend immediate, unlawful violence or recklessness as to whether such apprehension is caused. This was confirmed in *Savage (1991)*.

> **Exam tip**
>
> The significant issue is quite often that of 'immediacy' – for this, use either *Logdon* or *Smith* – what matters is what the victim thought the defendant might do next.

Battery

Revised ☐

- The *actus reus* is the application of unlawful force. There is no need to prove harm or pain. A mere touch can be sufficient, for example tickling, kissing or throwing water over someone. In *Collins v Willcock (1984)* it was held that 'any touching of another person, however slight, may amount to a battery'.

- In practice it would need to go beyond the ordinary physical contact that is part of ordinary life such as squeezing a hand so tightly that it hurts or repeatedly slapping someone on the back. It is clear from *Wilson v Pringle (1987)* that the touching has to be hostile to amount to a battery. In that case a schoolboy in fun seized a bag being carried over the shoulder by another pupil. Scratches and minor bruising are likely to be treated as battery, although there is no need for injury to be proved.

- It can be indirect as in *Fagan* – driving a car onto someone's foot – or *Thomas (1985)* – touching someone's clothes. In *DPP v K (1990)* it was battery when acid was put in a hot air hand drier and injured someone. In *Haystead (2000)* it was battery to a baby when a man punched a woman and she dropped the baby.

- The *mens rea* is intention or recklessness as to whether unlawful force will be applied. This was confirmed in *Venna (1976)*, where the court said that the defendant must intentionally or recklessly apply force to another.

Exam tip

If there has been any slight injury, i.e. injury other than minor bruising or scratches, consider actual bodily harm **s. 47 Offences Against the Person Act 1861** as well as battery.

S. 47 Actual bodily harm (ABH)   Revised

- This is defined in the Act as 'any assault occasioning actual bodily harm'.
- The *actus reus* is either assault or battery plus actual bodily harm.
- In *Miller (1954)* actual bodily harm includes 'any hurt or injury calculated to interfere with health or comfort'. It has to be more than 'transient or trifling'. Harm is not limited to injury to the skin, flesh and bones. In *Smith v DPP (2006)* it was held that cutting off a girl's ponytail amounted to ABH.
- ABH can include psychiatric injury, but in *Chan Fook (1994)* it was said that psychiatric injury 'does not include mere emotions such as fear or distress or panic'. There must be 'some identifiable clinical condition'.
- For the *mens rea*, only the *mens rea* for assault or battery is needed. For example in *Roberts* a man gave a girl a lift in his car and made sexual advances, touching her clothes. She feared rape and jumped from the car and was injured. He argued that he saw no risk of injury, but court said that it was sufficient that he had the *mens rea* for battery.
- Another example is *Savage*. In this case the defendant threw beer into the victim's face, which was battery, for which she had the *mens rea*. But she also let go of the glass and caused a cut to the victim's wrist, and was convicted of ABH and again the court said that it was sufficient that she had the *mens rea* for the battery.

Typical mistake

When explaining this offence, students often fail to explain the *actus reus* and the *mens rea* of either assault or (more usually) battery which is essential for this 'compound' offence.

Typical mistake

Note that one of the commonest mistakes made in exams is to explain that 'the *mens rea* for this offence is intention or recklessness as to causing ABH'.

S. 20 Wounding or inflicting grievous bodily harm   Revised

- This is defined as 'unlawfully and maliciously wounding and/or inflicting any grievous bodily harm upon any other person either with or without a weapon'.
- The *actus reus* is either inflicting GBH or wounding.
- GBH means serious harm as in *Saunders (1985)* and includes things like broken limbs, dislocations, permanent disability or scarring and substantial loss of blood.
- In *Bollom (2003)* where severe bruising was caused to a young child, the court held that the victim's age and state of health were relevant in deciding whether an injury amounted to GBH.
- It can include psychiatric injury as long as it is 'serious' (*Ireland* and *Burstow*).
- Inflict does not require direct contact as confirmed in *Burstow (1998)* and therefore in practice means the same as 'cause' in s. 18 of the Act. In *Martin (1881)* a man was found guilty of s. 20 when he shouted 'fire' in a crowded cinema and caused injury to people who were trampled in the panic to escape.
- Wounding means breaking the skin, not internal bleeding, as in *Eisenhower (1984)*. Any cut could therefore be treated as wounding.

Exam tip

Notice that GBH and wounding are separate *actus reus* elements and in your answer you should state whether the situation in the scenario is GBH or wounding. In some situations it will be both.

- In *Dica (2004)* a man was convicted of 'biological GBH' when he recklessly infected a woman with HIV when he had unprotected sex with her.
- The *mens rea* is intention or recklessness as to whether some harm caused. In *Mowatt (1968)* it was confirmed that the defendant merely has to foresee some physical harm, albeit of a minor character.

Typical mistake

Another very common exam mistake is to write that the *mens rea* for s. 20 is 'intention or recklessness as to causing GBH'.

S. 18 Wounding or causing grievous bodily harm with intent

Revised

- The *actus reus* of this offence is wounding or causing GBH. Because judges have decided that cause (s. 18) and inflict (s. 20) amount to the same thing, the *actus reus* of the two offences is identical. The difference between the two offences is entirely in the *mens rea*.
- The *mens rea* of s. 18 is either intention to cause GBH or intention to resist arrest. Intention is to act deliberately, to make something your aim and purpose *(Mohan)*. Intention can be direct or oblique which is where the defendant claims to have some other purpose, but the jury are satisfied that the defendant knew serious injury was virtually certain *(Nedrick/Woollin)*.

Exam tip

S. 18 is the only offence for which oblique intent is relevant. All the others have a *mens rea* which includes recklessness as an alternative to intention and recklessness will always be easier to prove than oblique intent.

Now test yourself 3

Tested

1 What is the *actus reus* of assault?
2 Which case confirmed that words can constitute assault?
3 Which case decided that 'immediate' could include more remote threats?
4 For battery, which case ruled that the infliction of unlawful personal violence had to be hostile?
5 Which case shows that battery can be indirect?
6 In s. 47 ABH, what is the definition in *R v Miller* of actual bodily harm?
7 Which case confirmed that the *mens rea* for s. 47 is the same as that for battery?
8 Which case defined wounding as an injury which breaks both the outer and inner skin?
9 What is the *mens rea* for s. 20 inflicting GBH and/or wounding?
10 Give three examples of serious harm.

Answers on p.134

Exam tip

If the injury is serious enough to be GBH, say that the *actus reus* is the same for both s. 20 and s. 18 and discuss whether the *actus reus* is met.

Remember that a cut that bleeds could amount to either s. 20 or s. 18, even if the injury does not appear to be serious. This needs to be discussed as wounding rather than GBH.

Next consider the *mens rea*. In most cases s. 20 will be the appropriate offence because it would be hard to prove that the defendant intended to cause serious harm, so outline and apply the *mens rea* of s. 20. If there is any suggestion that serious injury was intended (e.g. use of a weapon, repeated attack), consider s. 18 and discuss the *mens rea* of s. 18.

Check your understanding

1 Match the cases shown below the table with the facts and identify the relevant area of law.

Case	Facts	Area of law
	Newsagent and lottery ticket	
	Did not close gate	
	Aimed to get baby into pram	
	Tried to poison mother	
	Aimed to hit man but hit woman	
	Did not know there was a risk	
	Used girlfriend as shield	
	Did not know students were taking drugs	
	A swarm of bees	
	Woman jumped from moving car	
	Set fire to his bed	
	Thought victim was dead so threw him over cliff	
	Taxi driver killed	
	Refused blood transfusion	
	Original wound was still operating and substantial	

Smith	Roberts	Hill v Baxter	Miller
Pittwood	Pagett	Harrow v Shah	White
Hancock and Shankland	Cunningham	Latimer	Sweet v Parsley
Blaue	Thabo Meli	Woollin	

2 Add some detail to the basic definitions shown below. (To achieve high marks you will need more than just a simple definition of the *actus reus* and *mens rea* of the relevant offence.)

Assault	
	Actus reus is any act which makes the victim apprehend the immediate infliction of unlawful force.
Two pieces of detail:	
	Mens rea is an intention to cause the victim to apprehend immediate, unlawful violence or recklessness as to whether such apprehension is caused.
Definition of intention:	
Definition of recklessness:	

Battery	
	Actus reus is the application of unlawful force.
Two pieces of detail:	
	Mens rea is intention or recklessness as to applying unlawful force.
Definition of recklessness:	
Confirmed in:	

Actual bodily harm s. 47	
	Actus reus is either assault or battery plus actual bodily harm.
Two pieces of detail:	
	Mens rea – only the *mens rea* for assault or battery is needed.
Facts and conclusion in *Roberts*:	
Facts and conclusion in *Savage*.	

Grievous bodily harm and wounding s. 20	
	Actus reus is either inflicting GBH or wounding.
Meaning of GBH:	
Meaning of wounding:	
	Mens rea is intention or recklessness as to whether some harm caused.
Definition of intention:	
Definition of recklessness:	
Statement in *Mowatt*:	

Grievous bodily harm and wounding s. 18	
	Actus reus is either inflicting GBH or wounding.
Meaning of GBH:	
Meaning of wounding:	
	Mens rea is either intention to cause GBH or intention to resist arrest.
Definition of intention:	
Definition of oblique intent:	

Answers on p.134–35

Exam practice

Jason has organised a party at his home to celebrate his eighteenth birthday. Unfortunately, Dave and Mike, who were not invited, hear about this and decide to gate crash the party. When they enter the house, Jason asks them to leave but Dave refuses and threatens to 'see he suffers a nasty accident when they next play football'.

Jason picks up a beer glass and hits Dave over the head with it – the glass shatters and causes Dave to suffer serious cuts. One of these is a deep gash to his cheek which will probably leave a permanent scar.

1 Discuss Dave's criminal liability in respect of his behaviour towards Jason. [8 marks]

2 Discuss Jason's criminal liability for the injuries suffered by Dave. [8 marks]

Online

Exam summary

✔ You will be expected to explain the rules on some aspects of criminal liability. You must be prepared for questions on *actus reus*, including specific aspects such as voluntary acts, omissions and causation; *mens rea*, including transferred malice; the coincidence of *actus reus* and *mens rea*; and strict liability, including advantages and disadvantages.

✔ You might also have to apply the rules to a factual scenario. This is particularly likely with the rules on causation. But on one occasion the question required you to apply the rules on transferred malice.

✔ You will always have a scenario based on at least one non-fatal offence. Sometimes you will be told the offence, but often the question will refer to 'criminal liability' and you will have to identify the offence.

✔ You must be prepared to explain the *actus reus* and *mens rea* of assault, battery, s. 47 ABH, s. 20 GBH/ wounding and s. 18 GBH/wounding with intent. You will also have to apply the rules to the facts in the scenario.

✔ Remember to use authorities (cases and references to the Offences Against the Person Act 1861) to support your arguments.

10 The courts: procedure and sentencing

For this topic you need to understand:

- an outline of the criminal courts (Magistrates' and Crown)
- classification of offences – summary, indictable (triable either way and indictable only) in the context of non-fatal offences
- outline of the procedure to trial: bail, plea and sending for trial
- the burden and standard of proof that applies in criminal cases
- the aims of sentencing and the factors that might apply when sentencing adult offenders and the range of sentencing options open to the courts.

Courts that try criminal cases   Revised ☐

- The Magistrates' Court and the Crown Court are the two courts where someone charged with a criminal case may appear.
- The role each court plays depends on whether the case is summary, either way or indictable.

Classification of offences and outline procedure to trial   Revised ☐

Summary offence procedure

- After the defendant has been **arrested** and charged by the **police**, they can decide to release them on bail (Bail Act 1976) or keep them in custody whilst they make further inquiries. The **Crown Prosecution Service (CPS)** will advise the police whether there is enough evidence for the case to proceed based on the evidential and public interest tests.
- All summary offences, which are the least serious, are dealt with in the Magistrates' Court and the defendant may be represented for the first hearing by the **duty solicitor** at the court.
- The purpose of that hearing is for the defendant to enter a plea which could be guilty or not guilty. If a **guilty plea** is made, sentencing may take place immediately on first appearance or the Magistrates may adjourn for pre-sentencing reports before they pass sentence.
- However, if a **not guilty plea** is entered the procedure may be adjourned for witnesses or for the defendant to obtain further legal advice. The magistrates will also decide whether the defendant should receive **legal aid** and be released on **bail** or kept in custody

Either way offence procedure

- After the defendant has been arrested and charged by the police, they can decide to release them on bail (Bail Act 1976) or keep them in custody whilst they make further inquiries.

- The CPS will advise the police whether there is enough evidence for the case to proceed based on the evidential and public interest tests.

- All people charged with criminal offences first appear in the Magistrates' Court. They may be represented at the first hearing by the duty solicitor at the court.

- For **either way offences (mid-range)** there is a **plea before venue** and the defendant is asked whether they plead guilty or not guilty. If a guilty plea is entered the defendant may be sentenced or sent to the Crown Court if the magistrates don't have sufficient powers.

- If a not guilty plea is entered the magistrates will carry out a **mode of trial** hearing to decide if the case is to be heard at the Magistrates' or the Crown Court.

- If the defendant elects for Crown Court trial, or the magistrates decide that they do not have jurisdiction, the case will be sent to Crown Court for plea and directions hearing and then adjourned for trial by jury.

- If the defendant elects for trial before magistrates and magistrates have accepted jurisdiction, the case will be adjourned for trial. Also the magistrates will decide whether the defendant should receive legal aid and be released on bail or kept in custody

Indictable only offence procedure

- After the defendant has been arrested and charged by the police, they can decide to release the defendant on bail (Bail Act 1976) or keep them in custody whilst they make further inquiries. The CPS will advise the police whether there is enough evidence for the case to proceed based on the evidential and public interest tests.

- All people charged with criminal offences first appear in the Magistrates' Court. They may be represented by the duty solicitor at the court. The magistrates will decide whether the defendant should receive legal aid and be released on bail or kept in custody.

- For indictable offences, which are the most serious type of offences, the case is **transferred to Crown Court for a plea and directions hearing** under the Crime and Disorder Act 1998.

- If a guilty plea is entered the judge will pass sentence, after a possible adjournment for pre-sentence report.

- If the defendant pleads not guilty, the case is adjourned.

- A jury will decide on guilt/innocence and if the defendant is found guilty the judge will pass sentence.

Bail

- For all types of offence a decision has to be made about whether to remand a defendant in custody or release them on bail.

- Bail can be granted by the police or the courts. S. 4 of the Bail Act 1976 gives a general right to bail, but the court can refuse bail if the court has reasonable grounds to believe that there is a risk that the defendant might:
  - abscond and not attend their trial
  - commit a further offence if granted bail
  - interfere with/threaten witnesses.

> **Exam tip**
>
> Make sure you are clear which of the three types of offence you are being asked about. The procedure before trial will be different for each.

- The court can also take into account other factors like the nature of the offence and the defendant's previous record in deciding whether to grant bail.
- Bail can be unconditional or the court or police can attach conditions, such as surrender of passport, regular reporting to a police station, residence at a particular place or requirement for a surety.
- It is an offence for a defendant to fail to answer bail and attend their trial.

> **Exam tip**
>
> When answering questions on pre-trial procedures, make sure you are clear whether the offence being charged is summary, either way or indictable. The focus should be on first appearance at a Magistrates' Court, requests for bail and legal aid and the defendant's plea.

Burden and standard of proof — Revised

- Prosecution must prove guilt **beyond reasonable doubt**.
- This is the **standard of proof** and if the prosecution cannot prove their case to this standard the defendant will be acquitted.
- We say that the **burden of proof** is on the prosecution because it is they that have to prove their case, not the defence.

Now test yourself 1 — Tested

1. What are the three different types of offences?
2. Which Act regulates bail?
3. What is the Act's key provision regarding the granting of bail?
4. Give three examples where bail may be disallowed.
5. Give two examples of conditions which may be imposed for bail.
6. In either way offences, if the defendant pleads not guilty, does he/she have the right to be tried by magistrates?
7. Under which Act will magistrates automatically transfer the defendant to Crown Court for trial in indictable cases?
8. What is the standard of proof in criminal cases?

Answers on p.135

Sentencing — Revised

Aims of sentencing

Retribution

- This is the idea that if someone has broken the law they should be punished and get their 'just deserts' and receive the sentence their degree of fault deserves.
- To an extent all sentences involve retribution.

Deterrence

- There are two types of deterrence: **individual deterrence** aims to prevent the offender from reoffending and **general deterrence** aims to deter others.

Rehabilitation

- Rehabilitation aims to reform the offender. Some sentences, such as community sentences, have an obvious rehabilitative purpose.
- Educational and counselling services in prisons and special units to treat sexual and drug offenders are further examples of measures designed to reform the defendant's behaviour and help reintegration back into society.

Protection of society

- It is obvious that the public need protecting from dangerous criminals and custody is the sentence used in these cases.
- Under the Criminal Justice Act 2003, extended sentences are possible in cases where there is significant risk to the public.

Reparation

- Increasingly there is an emphasis in sentencing on the needs and feelings of victims and on trying to ensure that the offender makes amends.
- This might be through a compensation order or through a community order involving some kind of reparative work.

Factors in sentencing

- In deciding on a sentence the court will take a number of things into account, such as the maximum sentence allowed for the offence. Note that the maximum period of custody is rarely given and often any kind of prison sentence would be inappropriate.
- The maximum prison sentences for assault and battery are six months; for s. 47 and s. 20 five years; and for s. 18 life.
- Sentencing guidelines are issued by the **Sentencing Guidelines Council** which set out the starting point and the range of sentencing options for an offence and the kind of factors the court should consider. They may suggest a '**tariff**', which is the sentence appropriate for the 'average' example of the offence.
- The offender's background and any **aggravating**/**mitigating** factors will be taken into account. This may involve referring to a pre-sentence report drawn up by the probation service or to medical or psychiatric reports, if appropriate.

Aggravating and mitigating factors in sentencing

- These are the range of factors the courts may take into account before sentencing.
- Aggravating factors are things that make the offence more serious. Examples in the Criminal Justice Act 2003 include:
  - previous convictions for similar offences
  - offences committed whilst on bail
  - offences that involve racist or religious hostility or on the grounds of disability or sexuality
  - offence against a vulnerable victim (e.g. young, elderly or disabled)
  - offence committed by a group (e.g. a gang)
  - offence involving an abuse of trust (e.g. sexual assault by a doctor; theft by a bank cashier)
  - use of a weapon
  - repeated attacks
  - offences committed whilst under the influence of alcohol or drugs.
- Mitigating factors are circumstances which allow the court to impose a lower sentence. Examples in the Criminal Justice Act 2003 include:
  - first offence
  - defendant is very young or old
  - defendant is a vulnerable offender and easily influenced

> **Typical mistake**
>
> Students often confuse aims of sentencing with factors and types. Make sure you read the question carefully and are clear about what you are being asked.

– defendant has expressed remorse and made efforts to compensate the victim
– defendant has difficult circumstances
– pleading guilty at the first opportunity reduces a sentence by one third
– provocation by the victim.

Range of sentences available to the courts

Custodial sentences

● These involve **imprisonment, either immediate or suspended** (i.e. when the sentence is not activated unless the defendant commits further offences).

● Imprisonment can be for a fixed term or for an indeterminate period.

Community sentences

● The Criminal Justice Act 2003 allows for a community order which can include any requirements the court sees as necessary, reflecting the seriousness of the offence.

Community orders

● These can include **community punishment orders** (where the offender has to carry out unpaid work (from 40–300 hours over a year), **community rehabilitation orders** (which place the offender under the supervision of a probation officer), **curfew requirements** and **alcohol/drug treatment**.

Financial sentences

● These include **fines**, which can be enforced through an attachment of earnings order.

● **Compensation orders** can be made for injuries or property damage.

Discharge

● **Discharges may be Absolute or Conditional** (if the offender commits a further offence in the stated period, then they can be resentenced for the original offence).

> **Exam tip**
>
> If you are asked to comment on the *factors* that would be considered in sentencing the defendant, be sure to include any of the aggravating and mitigating factors which are relevant to the facts of the scenario.

Now test yourself 2

Tested ☐

1 Name three different aims of sentencing.
2 What is a suspended sentence?
3 Give three examples of a community sentence.
4 What are the two types of discharge?
5 Give three examples of mitigating factors.
6 Give three examples of aggravating factors.

Answers on p.135

Check your understanding

1   In the table write three points about the criminal procedure for each of the types of offence.

Summary offences	
Point 1	
Point 2	
Point 3	
Either way offences	
Point 1	
Point 2	
Point 3	
Indictable offences	
Point 1	
Point 2	
Point 3	

2   Write simple definitions for the sentencing terms shown below.

Term	Definition
Retribution	
Individual deterrence	
General deterrence	
Rehabilitation	
Tariff	
Aggravating	
Mitigating	
Custody	
Suspended sentence	
Conditional discharge	

Answers on p.135–6

Exam practice

Jason has organised a party at his home to celebrate his eighteenth birthday. Unfortunately, Dave and Mike, who were not invited, hear about this and decide to gate crash the party. When they enter the house, Jason asks them to leave, but Dave refuses and threatens to 'see he suffers a nasty accident when they next play football'.

Jason picks up a beer glass and hits Dave over the head with it – the glass shatters and causes Dave to suffer serious cuts. One of these is a deep gash to his cheek which will probably leave a permanent scar.

1   Outline the pre-trial procedure which would be followed if Dave were to be charged with assault
    (a summary offence).   **[5 marks]**

2   Assuming that Dave is convicted of an offence, briefly outline the factors which the court would
    take into account before he is sentenced.   **[5 marks]**

Online

Exam summary

✔ Be prepared to briefly outline the procedure to trial for summary, either way and indictable offences. Make sure you identify the courts correctly.

✔ You could be asked to explain the rules on bail.

✔ There will be a question on sentencing; it might be on aims, the range of sentences available or the factors considered when a person is sentenced. You will be required to apply the rules to a person in a factual scenario.

11 Liability in negligence

For this topic you need to understand the basic principles of the tort of negligence:

- the basic principles of the tort of negligence
- duty of care including the neighbour principle and the Caparo three-part test
- breach of duty including the concept of the reasonable man and the risk factors
- damage including causation of damage and remoteness.

Basic principles of the tort of negligence   Revised

- Torts are civil wrongs, which entitle victims to claim compensation.
- The most important is the tort of negligence which arises in a variety of situations involving injury or damage caused by careless behaviour.
- In order to succeed in a claim for negligence, it must be proved that the victim is owed a duty of care, that there is breach of duty and that relevant damage or injury has been caused.

Duty of care   Revised

- Duty of Care was defined first in *Donoghue v Stevenson (1932)* as the 'neighbour principle' meaning that you **owe a duty to avoid acts or omissions which you can reasonably foresee might affect your neighbour, who is anyone you can reasonably foresee might be affected by what you do**.
- In order to put a limit on the number of possible claims, the neighbour principle was modified by the three-part test in *Caparo v Dickman (1990)*. Now in deciding whether a duty of care is owed, a three-part test is applied.

Caparo three-part test

Was loss/damage reasonably foreseeable?

- In *Jolley v Sutton Borough Council (2000)* it was foreseeable that boys would try and repair an old boat on council-owned land and be injured by it.
- In *Langley v Dray (1998)* it was foreseeable that police chasing a speeding car might be exposed to the risk of injury by increasing their speed to keep up with it.

Was there sufficient proximity?

- This means was the victim sufficiently close in terms of time or distance or relationship? In *Bourhill v Young (1943)* the claimant was not in the immediate vicinity of the accident (she heard the sound, but

Key terms

Duty of care is the idea that someone has a responsibility to avoid acting in a way that might cause injury or damage to someone they should have realised might have been affected by their actions. It is usually defined as the neighbour principle.

The neighbour principle is that you owe a duty to avoid acts or omissions which you can reasonably foresee might affect your neighbour, who is anyone you can reasonably foresee might be affected by what you do.

Exam tip

Although an 'explanation' question on duty of care can be answered effectively by explaining the Caparo incremental approach (three-part test), some reference to the 'neighbour principle' is always creditworthy.

because she was behind a tram she could not see it) and so was not owed a duty of care.

- In *McLoughlin v O'Brian (1983)* however, the claimant was told of a serious accident involving her husband and children. She was not at the scene of the accident and went straight to the hospital and suffered nervous shock as a result of what she saw and was told there. There was no proximity in terms of time or space, but a duty was owed because of proximity of relationship.

Is it fair, just and reasonable to impose a duty of care?

- In some circumstances it would be unhelpful for society to allow a duty of care to be owed.

- In *Alcock v Chief Constable of South Yorkshire (1992)*, relatives who suffered nervous shock from watching the Hillsborough disaster on TV were not owed a duty of care because it would open up the possibility of too many claims. This is the 'floodgates argument'.

- A recent example is *Mitchell v Glasgow City Council (2009)*, in which a council tenant killed his neighbour following a meeting with the council at which he had been warned about his behaviour towards the neighbour. The court decided that it would not be fair, just and reasonable for the council to owe a duty of care to the neighbour because it might lead to a flood of claims affecting other public officials.

> **Exam tip**
>
> There only has to be reasonable foreseeability of *some* harm or property damage if the defendant does not take reasonable care. The precise form of injury or damage need not be foreseeable.

> **Exam tip**
>
> In explaining the meaning of duty of care, you must include a brief description of a relevant case for each of the three headings described. The policy test is often the weakest part of an answer – learn the key points carefully.

Breach of duty

Revised

Concept of the reasonable man

- The test used to decide whether there is a breach of duty is whether the defendant behaved as a prudent and reasonable person would have – the concept of the 'reasonable man'.

- This principle was set out in *Blyth v Birmingham Waterworks Co (1856)*. If the defendant's **behaviour falls below the standard of the reasonable person** then they are in breach of duty.

- In *Nettleship v Weston (1971)* it was decided that the defendant is compared with a person of average skill. In that case, a learner driver was measured against an average driver, i.e. an experienced driver.

- If the defendant is a professional person and has special skills, they are compared to an **average experienced person** in that profession.

- In *Bolam v Friern Hospital Management Committee (1957)* a doctor was not in breach of duty if he followed standard procedures supported by a reasonable body of medical opinion.

- In *Wells v Cooper (1958)* the defendant was a DIY enthusiast who fixed a new handle to his back door. His duty was to fit the handle to the standard of a reasonably competent amateur.

- The conduct of a child is compared to that expected of a reasonable child of the same age. In *Mullins v Richards (1998)* two fifteen-year-old girls were playing with plastic rulers, one of which broke and blinded one of the girls. The court decided that a reasonable fifteen-year-old would not have foreseen this risk of harm.

> **Typical mistake**
>
> Students often fail to recognise that the reasonable man has different characteristics, for example, if a professional or a child.
>
> Some students also confuse the reasonable man test and the risk factors.

> **Key terms**
>
> Breach of duty is the idea that someone who owes a duty of care has behaved in a way that falls below the standard of the reasonable person.

Factors to decide whether a person has acted reasonably

Probability of harm

- More care would need to be taken with something that is quite likely to happen.

- In *Bolton v Stone (1951)* a cricket ball was hit out of the ground and over a 17-foot high fence only 6 times in 30 years and no one had ever been injured. The reasonable person would assume that the risk of injury was low.

- Contrast this with *Haley v London Electricity Board (1964)*. In this case a hammer was left on the pavement to warn people of excavations. This was sufficient for sighted people, but Mr Haley was blind and he tripped over it. The number of blind people is large enough for the defendant to have realised that this kind of incident was quite probable.

Magnitude of risk

- The court also has to consider how serious an injury could potentially be. The more serious the likely consequences, the more care needs to be taken.

- In *Paris v Stepney BC (1951)* for example, because Mr Paris was blind in one eye, greater care should have been taken to ensure that he used protective goggles. He was blinded by a piece of molten metal.

Cost and practicality of taking precautions

- If the cost of taking precautions to eliminate the risk is too great, the defendant will not be in breach of duty.

- For example in *Latimer v AEC (1953)* a factory became flooded and sawdust was put on the floor to stop workers slipping. The only way to have been sure no one would be injured would be to close the factory. It was unreasonable to expect the owners to do this.

Possible benefits of the risk

- There are some risks that have benefits for society (also known as social utility of the risk). For example if all cars ran at 5mph, there would be fewer accidents, but it would be difficult for society to function properly.

- In *Watt v Hertfordshire CC (1954)* a fireman was injured because equipment was being carried in a fire engine not adapted to carry such equipment. Because it was an emergency call and the specialist fire engine was on another call, the benefits of being able to save a victim trapped under a vehicle outweighed the risks resulting from moving the equipment in an unsuitable fire engine.

> **Exam tip**
>
> When answering a problem-solving question on breach of duty, the key focus is whether, in the circumstances, the defendant acted as 'the reasonable man' would have. First consider if there are any relevant issues concerning the defendant (e.g. age, profession or learner) and then address the relevant risk factors, especially probability of harm, how serious that harm could be and the practicality and cost of taking precautions – these are *always* relevant factors.

Damage — Revised

- The person claiming must be able to prove that they have suffered damage or injury, that the defendant has caused the damage and the damage is not too remote.

Defendant must have caused loss/damage

- The question must be asked whether the injury/loss would have occurred 'but for' the defendant's actions.
- In *Barnett v Chelsea Hospital (1968)* the patient would have died anyway (of arsenic poisoning), even if the treatment had not been negligent.

Damage must not be too remote

- This means that the type of damage must be reasonably foreseeable.
- In the *Wagon Mound (1961)* it was reasonably foreseeable that spilled oil would cause pollution, but it was not foreseeable that it would be ignited on the other side of the harbour and damage a wharf.
- In *Doughty v Turner Engineering (1964)* the defendant was not liable when an asbestos cover was accidentally dropped into some molten liquid. The resulting eruption of the liquid was not foreseeable and therefore too remote.
- Note that as long as the type of damage is reasonably foreseeable, it does not matter if the damage occurs in an unforeseeable way. In *Hughes v Lord Advocate (1963)* it was foreseeable that paraffin lamps left unattended would cause burns; it did not matter that the burns were caused by an explosion which was not reasonably foreseeable.
- The **thin skull rule** also applies. In *Smith v Leech Brain (1961)* molten metal caused a burn, which unexpectedly led to cancer because it triggered the victim's pre-cancerous condition. However, you must take your victim as you find him and as long as the type of injury is foreseeable (in this case a burn), the defendant would be liable for all the consequences, even if they are worse than would be normally expected.

> **Typical mistake**
>
> Students often refer to criminal rather than tort cases when discussing causation and the thin skull rule.

> **Key terms**
>
> Damage is remote if it is of a kind that is not foreseeable, e.g. pollution damage might be foreseeable, but not fire damage (*Wagon Mound*).

> **Exam tip**
>
> When explaining remoteness of damages, include the tests from *Hughes v Lord Advocate* and *Smith v Leech Brain* to ensure high marks.

Now test yourself 1

Tested ▢

1. What is the 'neighbour principle' from *Donoghue v Stevenson*?
2. What are the three rules in the incremental approach from *Caparo v Dickman*?
3. Why did the House of Lords use the policy test in *Alcock v Chief Constable of South Yorkshire*?
4. Which case defined the 'reasonable man test' used for breach of duty?
5. What rule for medical negligence cases was laid down in *Bolam v Friern Barnet HMC*?
6. What rule was derived from *Mullins v Richards*?
7. Name any three risk factors which will be considered in applying the 'reasonable man' test.
8. In *Barnett v Chelsea and Kensington HMC*, why was the hospital not liable for the doctor's clear breach of duty?
9. What rule is illustrated by *Hughes v Lord Advocate*?

Answers on p.136

Check your understanding

1 In the table below, identify the case being referred to and which area of law it applies to.

Facts	Name of case	Area of law
He should have been made to wear goggles		
To close the factory would be disproportionate		
Injured by cricket ball		
Injured chasing stolen car		
He would have died anyway		
A learner driver		
Not sufficient warning for the blind		
It was not foreseeable that it would ignite		
She was not in the immediate vicinity		
Decomposed snail		
Burn caused cancer		
Introduced three-part test		

2 Use the word bank to fill in the missing words in this paragraph about the meaning of the term breach of duty.

Once duty of care has been proved, we must then prove that the defendant has breached their duty. To do this, we compare the defendant to the _____ person. If they have not acted as an ordinary _____ person would have done, they have breached their duty. In *Nettleship v Weston*, a _____ driver breached his duty because his driving was worse than an ordinary driver's; it was irrelevant that he was a learner.

If the defendant is a _____ person and has special _____ in his/her job, he/she is compared to a _____ person in that profession (Bolam principle).

There are four _____ factors which can be used to make this comparison.

If there is a high degree of _____that harm or damage will result (if harm is likely), the reasonable person would take extra care. In *Bolton v Stone*, cricket balls only escaped from the cricket ground six times in _____ years, so no extra care needed to be taken.

If any harm is likely to occur and be serious (the _____ of likely harm), more precautions should be taken. Any harm to the one-eyed welder's eye would obviously be serious, so _____ should have been offered.

Cost is balanced against _____ If the risk is cheap and easy to prevent, the reasonable person would prevent it. In *Latimer v AEC Ltd*, it was impractical and too _____ to expect the factory to close when oil and water flooded the floor.

Sometimes risks are justified for the potential _____ they bring, such as saving life or limb. In *Watt v Hertfordshire CC*, taking specialist equipment on a fire engine not suitable for it was a risk worth taking if they could get to an accident scene more quickly and _____ a life.

practicality	competent	prudent	risk	learner
probability	professional	magnitude	thirty	skills
reasonable	protection	expensive	save	benefits

Answers on p.137

Exam practice

Mary is a customer at Great Value supermarket. She is walking beside the wine department when John, a newly employed shelf-stacker, approaches pushing a heavily-loaded trolley with cases of wine. Because he has almost finished his shift, John is pushing the trolley quite fast. When John is alongside Mary, a case of wine falls from the trolley and one bottle strikes Mary, causing a broken cheek bone. As a result, she has to attend hospital where she is told to stay off work for at least two weeks to recover. She also has to cancel a holiday that she was due to go on.

1 Briefly explain what the tests are to decide whether a duty of care is owed and discuss whether John owed Mary a duty of care. **[8 marks]**

2 Assuming that John did owe Mary a duty of care, discuss whether he was in breach of that duty. **[8 marks]**

Online

Exam summary

✔ You will be expected to explain the rules of the tort of negligence; duty of care; breach of duty, including the reasonable man test and the risk factors; damage, including factual causation and remoteness of damage.

✔ If you are asked about remoteness, refer to cases like the *Wagon Mound* and to *Hughes v Lord Advocate* and the thin skull rule.

✔ In breach of duty you may be asked to explain a specific number of risk factors, but not the reasonable man test. But note that you will need to refer to the reasonable man test in a later question if it asks you to discuss whether in the scenario someone was in breach of duty.

✔ You will also have to apply some of these rules to a factual scenario.

✔ Remember to use cases to support your arguments.

12 The courts: procedure and damages

For this topic you need to understand:

- the burden and standard of proof in negligence cases including *res ipsa loquitur*
- the purpose of damages and how damages are calculated
- the Civil Courts, procedure to trial and the three tracks
- opportunities for civil dispute resolution.

Burden and standard of proof Revised ☐

- In most civil cases, the burden of proof is on the claimant to prove his or her case against the defendant. But if *res ipsa loquitur* is alleged, the burden is then on the defendant to demonstrate that there is another plausible explanation for the situation. If they are able to do this, the burden then returns to the claimant to prove that this plausible explanation does not apply and that the defendant is negligent.
- The standard of proof is **'on the balance of probabilities'**, a lower standard than in criminal cases.

Res ipsa loquitur

- *Res ipsa loquitur* means 'the thing speaks for itself'. It applies when:
  - the events are under the control of the defendant
  - the events would not have occurred unless there had been negligence
  - there is no other explanation for the events.
- The claimant argues that on the face of it, the events could only have happened because of negligence. The defendant will be liable unless they can rebut the assumption with a plausible explanation. The burden of proof will therefore shift to the defendant.
- In *Scott v London and St Katherine's Docks (1865)* a bag of sugar fell on someone from the defendant's warehouse window. This could only have happened because of negligence.
- In *Mohan v Osborne (1938)* swabs were left in a patient after an operation. This could only have happened because of negligence during the operation.
- But in *Ratcliffe v Plymouth and Torbay HA (1998)*, the claimant said that injury to the spinal cord must have been caused by negligence – the facts speak for themselves – it must have been caused by the spinal anaesthetic. Health Authority rebuttal was that the claimant might have an unusual condition which caused the damage when the injection was given. The claimant was unable to prove negligence and the case failed.

> **Exam tip**
>
> Only include a discussion of the *res ipsa loquitur* rules if the question specifically requires you to do so.

> **Exam tip**
>
> When explaining the meaning of *res ipsa loquitur* it is important to mention that the effect of *res ipsa loquitur* is that the burden of proof is transferred from the claimant to the defendant.

Purpose of compensatory damages

- Damages in negligence are **compensatory**. The purpose of damages is to try to put the claimant in the position they were in before the tort was committed.
- Claimants are expected to follow the principle of **mitigation of loss**. This means that there is a general duty on all claimants to do what they reasonably can do to minimise their losses. For example, if a car is written off, the owner might be expected to replace it fairly quickly rather than hire a car for many weeks.

Key terms

Damages are the payment of money in compensation for losses or injury suffered.

Calculation of damages

- Damages are divided into **special damages** and **general damages**.

Special damages

- These cover quantifiable financial losses (**pecuniary damages**). It is easy to calculate exact amounts because they are actual losses from the date of the tort up to the date of trial, such as loss of earnings and medical expenses.
- Pecuniary damages cover any services, treatment or medical appliances, or the unpaid services of relatives or friends.
- Only reasonable expenses are recoverable. In *Cunningham v Harrison (1973)*, the claimant said that he needed a housekeeper and two nurses to live in his home and look after him. This claim was considered unreasonably large.
- The cost of special appliances like lifts to take wheelchairs in and out of cars can be claimed, as in *Povey v Rydal School (1970)*.

Key terms

Special damages are losses up to the date of the trial which can be precisely calculated.

General damages are future losses which cannot be precisely calculated.

Pecuniary losses are financial losses, e.g. costs incurred or loss of earnings.

Non-pecuniary damages are things that do not involve financial loss, e.g. loss of amenity or pain and suffering.

General damages

- These cover non-quantifiable losses. They are not easy to calculate because they are future losses. They are divided into two types: **pecuniary** and **non-pecuniary damages**.
- Pecuniary damages: the main element is future loss of earnings and is calculated by multiplying the average annual earnings lost (**multiplicand**) and the number of years of loss (**multiplier**). The maximum multiplier is 18. It also covers future medical expenses.
- Non-pecuniary damages: covers pain and suffering and the injury itself. It also covers loss of amenity (e.g. inability to enjoy life through damage to senses as in *West v Shephard (1963)*). It includes inability to run or walk, drive, do housework, shave, play sports or musical instruments.
- The award of damages will be reduced if the claimant receives financial support from sources like social security benefits.

Exam tip

Make sure you know the difference between special and general damages. A typical mistake is to confuse them and then to fail to identify the separate heads of damages for each.

Exam tip

If a 'damages' question requires you to explain and then apply the rules of damages to a scenario, decide what particular heads of damages are applicable and ensure these are fully explained and then applied. Heads of damages that are irrelevant to the scenario need only be identified briefly.

Payments

Provisional damages

- Generally only one award of damages can be made as a lump sum, but the court can make a provisional award allowing the claimant to return to court if their condition deteriorates.

Structured settlements

- These are covered by the Damages Act 1996.
- It is common for a structured settlement to be agreed where the money is invested and the claimant receives regular instalments.

Death of the victim

- If the victim dies before being able to claim damages, their estate can claim for losses through the victim's legal representative.

Contributory negligence

- Where the claimant is partly to blame for their injuries/damage, their damages are reduced (Law Reform (Contributory Negligence) Act 1945).

- In *Froom v Butcher (1976)* damages were reduced by 15–25 per cent for not wearing a seat belt.

The Civil Courts and procedure to trial

Revised

- The two Civil Courts in which a negligence claim might be brought are the County Court and the High Court.

How a civil action starts

- Personal injury claims of less than £50,000 and damage to property claims of less than £25,000 usually start in the County Court; above these figures they would start in the High Court (Queen's Bench Division).

- The person who starts the action is called the claimant and they issue a Claim Form.

- There is a court fee which increases with the size of claim. In 2007 the minimum was £30 up to a maximum of £1700 (claims over £300,000).

- The person who is sued by the claimant is called the defendant.

Options for the defendant

- When the Claim Form is served on the defendant (i.e. when they receive it), they have a number of options:
  - Admit the claim and pay the money.
  - Defend the claim – if they do this they must serve a defence.
  - If the defendant does nothing then after fourteen days the claimant can apply for a default judgment – the defendant will have to pay the full amount.
  - Lodge a counter-claim against the claimant.

The tracks

Revised

- There are three tracks that a civil case could be allocated to: small claims, fast track and multi-track.

Small claims track

- For claims up to £10,000 (personal injury claims up to £1000).

- There is a flexible informal procedure and no orders for costs, to encourage people to represent themselves.

Fast track

- This is for straightforward cases from £10,000 to £25,000 or personal injury claims over £1000.

- There is a preliminary hearing to lay down a timetable. Cases are put on a strict timetable and must be heard in 30 weeks.

> **Exam tip**
>
> If the scenario indicates that damages are for personal injury, make sure you say that above £1,000 the case would be allocated to the Fast Track, whereas claims for property damage would only go to the Fast Track if they were above £10,000.

Multi-track

- For claims over £25,000 or for complex cases below that amount.
- In the County Court they are heard by a Circuit judge who will manage the case to speed it up and save costs.
- All cases over £50,000 have to be heard in the High Court and some complex cases over £25,000 will be heard there.
- The multi-track is the only track used in the High Court.
- There will be a case management hearing where the judge will impose a timetable for procedural issues to be resolved.

Alternative dispute resolution

Revised

- The vast majority of cases are settled and do not go to court.
- Of those that go to court, most are settled before coming to trial.
- People are encouraged to use other forms of civil dispute resolution.
- If one of the parties unreasonably refuses to consider this option, the court has the power to disallow legal costs, as happened in *Dunnett v Railtrack (2002)*.
- The types of alternative dispute resolution available are:
  - negotiation – the parties try and reach agreement together
  - mediation – a go-between will help the parties reach agreement
  - conciliation – a go-between will offer advice or a solution, which the parties can accept or reject.

Now test yourself 1

Tested

1 What are special damages?
2 How are future losses of earnings calculated?
3 What are the three headings for non-pecuniary damages?
4 What does mitigation of loss require?
5 Saif has been injured in a car crash and compensation is estimated at £1500. Which track would he use and which court would hear his claim?
6 Fred is suing Jones the Builders for breach of contract and his losses are estimated at £6500. Which track would he use and which court would hear his claim?
7 Which case demonstrates that litigants have to consider other forms of civil dispute resolution seriously before initiating court-based action?
8 What are the three civil dispute resolution options open to the parties to use?
9 Which case established *res ipsa loquitur*?
10 What happens to the burden of proof if *res ipsa loquitur* is accepted by the trial judge?
11 What is the standard of proof in civil cases?

Answers on p.137

Check your understanding

1 Complete the tables below.

Special damages	
What they are	
What they cover	

General damages	
What they are	
Pecuniary	
Non-pecuniary	

Answers on p.137

Exam practice

Mary is a customer at Great Value supermarket. She is walking beside the wine department when John, a newly employed shelf-stacker, approaches pushing a heavily-loaded trolley with cases of wine. Because he has almost finished his shift, John is pushing the trolley quite fast. When John is alongside Mary, a case of wine falls from the trolley and one bottle strikes Mary, causing a broken cheek bone. As a result, she has to attend hospital where she is told to stay off work for at least two weeks to recover. She also has to cancel a holiday that she was due to go on.

1 Briefly explain how a court calculates an award of damages, and explain what types of damages
   Mary may be able to claim.   [8 marks]

2 Identify the court and track most likely to be used in a claim by Mary against John.   [5 marks]

Online

Exam summary

✔ You could be asked to describe the procedure in a negligence case up to trial or the question may focus on the courts/tracks that would hear such a case.

✔ Make sure you know the financial limits for the tracks. The question may refer you to the scenario and ask you to decide the most likely track.

✔ You will also have to explain how damages are calculated and apply the rules to a scenario. Don't forget to mention the purpose of damages.

✔ There may be a question on burden of proof and/ or on *res ipsa loquitur*. Make sure you know how this works and what its effect on the burden of proof would be.

13 Formation of contract

For this topic you need to understand:

- what a contract is and how it is formed
- offers and invitations to treat
- acceptance
- consideration
- intention to create legal relations.

Formation of contract   Revised ☐

- A contract can be defined as a legally binding agreement. In other words, it is an agreement that is recognised as having legal consequences.
- In order to be valid, a contract must meet certain conditions and these have to be present when it is formed.
- There can be several parties to a contract and contracts can be made by individuals, groups or organisations.
- Most contracts involve one party making an offer and another party indicating acceptance either verbally or in writing. These are known as **bilateral contracts** because for the contract to be valid, both parties must promise something.
- There are also **unilateral contracts**, where one party makes an offer but acceptance is through the performance of an act rather than through a formal indication of acceptance.
- A valid contract requires one party to make an **offer** and another party to accept that offer. This then becomes an **agreement**.

> **Key terms**
> A contract is a legally binding agreement, i.e. an agreement that can be enforced in the courts.

Offers and invitations to treat   Revised ☐

Offers

- An offer has been defined as an expression of willingness to contract on certain terms, made with the intention that it will become binding on acceptance.
- An offer can be specific – made to one person or a group of people – in which case it can only be accepted by that person or group.
- However, an offer can also be general and not limited in whom it is directed at. An offer of a reward is a good example. This could be accepted by anyone who meets the conditions.
- An offer may have time limits attached, in which case it can only be accepted during that time period. Offers without time limits are open for a 'reasonable time'.

> **Key terms**
> An offer is an expression of a willingness to enter into a legally binding agreement.

Types of offers

Reward posters/advertisements

- In some circumstances, these can constitute an offer. Offers must be firm, capable of being accepted and clear in requiring certain conditions to be fulfilled.

- In *Carlill v Carbolic Smoke Ball Co. (1893)*, the company issued a newspaper advertisement in which it said it would pay £100 to any person who contracted influenza after using one of its smoke balls in a specified manner for a specified period. This was a valid offer.

Promotional campaigns

- A supermarket might encourage customers to buy one product and get another product free, or it might offer two items for the price of one. As with reward posters, all that is required is that certain conditions are fulfilled.

> **Exam tip**
>
> Almost all the rules of contract law are common law, i.e. they derive from cases. In your answers you should refer to the cases which are authorities for the rules.

Rules of offers

- The offer must be certain. This means that its terms must be clear and definite, without any ambiguity.

- The offer may be made by any method. There is no requirement that an offer is in a particular form. It can be made in writing, verbally or by conduct (e.g. by picking up an item and taking it to the cash desk).

- The offer can be made to anyone. It can be made to an individual, a group, a company or an organisation, and even, as in *Carlill v Carbolic Smoke Ball Co.*, to the whole world.

- The offer must be communicated. A person cannot accept what he or she does not know about. An example might be an offer of a reward for the return of a missing dog. If someone finds the dog and returns it, but that person did not know about the reward, then technically he or she is not entitled to the reward because the offer was never received and therefore cannot be accepted.

- The offer must still be in existence when it is accepted. If a time limit is attached the offer will cease to exist on expiry of the time limit. An offer may also have been terminated.

Termination of offers

An offer can be brought to an end at any point before acceptance in a number of ways:

- Acceptance of the offer.

- Refusal of the offer.

- Counter-offer: in *Hyde v Wrench (1840)*, Wrench offered to sell his farm to Hyde for £1000. Hyde offered to pay £950, which Wrench rejected. When Hyde then tried to accept the original offer, it was held that his counter-offer of £950 had ended that offer. All the terms of an offer must be accepted, and an attempt to change any of them becomes a counter-offer.

- Revocation (withdrawal of the offer) must be communicated, though this could be by a third party, as in *Dickinson v Dodds (1876)*. The revocation must be received before the acceptance is made.

- In *Byrne v Van Tienhoven (1880)*, Van Tienhoven wrote to Byrne, making an offer, but changed his mind and wrote again to Byrne, withdrawing his offer. However, Byrne accepted the offer in a telegram, before he received the revocation letter, and therefore the acceptance was valid.

- Lapse of time: where no time limit is specified, the offer will remain open for a reasonable time. What is a reasonable time will depend on the circumstances. For example, an offer to sell perishable goods may lapse in a few days, while an offer to sell land would last considerably longer.
- In *Ramsgate Victoria Hotel v Montefiore (1866)*, an offer to buy shares in June had lapsed by November. If a time limit is specified, it must be complied with.

Invitations to treat

- An invitation to treat is an invitation to someone to make an offer. Whether something is an offer or an invitation depends on the circumstances.

Types of invitations to treat

- Displays of goods in shop windows: in *Fisher v Bell (1961)*, a prosecution under the Offensive Weapons Act 1959 failed because the offence was to offer for sale prohibited weapons. Although the shopkeeper was displaying a flick knife in his window with a price tag, the court decided that this amounted to an invitation to treat and not an offer for sale.
- Goods on display in supermarkets and self-service stores: this principle was established in *Pharmaceutical Society of Great Britain v Boots (1953)*.
- Small advertisements (e.g. in magazines or newspapers): in *Partridge v Crittenden (1968)*, an advertisement of wild birds for sale was found to be an invitation, not an offer, so a prosecution for offering for sale a wild bird under the Protection of Birds Act 1954 failed.
- Price lists, catalogues, etc.
- Responses to requests for information: in *Harvey v Facey (1893)*, Harvey telegraphed Facey and asked: 'Will you sell me Bumper Hall Pen? Telegraph lowest cash price.' Facey replied by telegram: 'Lowest cash price for Bumper Hall Pen £900.' It was held that Facey's telegram was not an offer but merely a statement of the price.
- Auction sales: confirmed in *British Car Auctions v Wright (1972)*, the offer is made by the person making the bid.
- Invitations to tender: the person inviting the tenders is free to accept any of the tenders, and not necessarily the cheapest.

> **Exam tip**
>
> An exam question may ask you to say what an offer is or it may ask about specific aspects of an offer, e.g. ways in which it can come to an end. You should illustrate your answer by referring to cases.

> **Key terms**
>
> An invitation to treat is an invitation to someone to make an offer.

> **Exam tip**
>
> You must be able to distinguish between an offer and an invitation to treat. The significance of the distinction is that if an offer is made, all that is required from the other party is an acceptance. However, if there is an invitation to treat, the other party has to make an offer, which leaves the person who issued the invitation able to decide whether or not to accept the offer. A popular exam question is one in which you are asked to distinguish between an offer and an invitation to treat.

Acceptance   Revised ☐

- Acceptance is unqualified and unconditional agreement to all the terms of the offer by words or conduct. If conditions or qualifications are added, a counter-offer is created.
- Acceptance must be communicated. In *Felthouse v Bindley (1862)*, the claimant offered to buy a horse from his nephew, adding: 'If I hear no more about him, I shall consider the horse mine.' The court refused to regard the defendant's silence as acceptance.

- Acceptance can be inferred from conduct. The principle seems to be that when you start to implement what is in the offer, you have accepted it.
- If a method of acceptance is specified, it must be complied with. However, in some circumstances another, equally good method might suffice (*Tinn v Hoffman*, 1873).
- If no method is specified, any method will do, as long as it is effective.
- The **'postal rule'** applies when the ordinary postal system is used. Acceptance is valid when posted, even if the letter is lost in the post. Revocation is valid when received. In *Household Fire Insurance v Grant* (1879), a letter was lost in the post; nevertheless, there was a proper acceptance and a binding contract.
- When **instantaneous methods** are used, acceptance is immediate as long as it is communicated. Such methods include telephone, fax and email and acceptance is immediate as long as it gets through.
- In *Entores v Miles Far East* (1955), an English company in London was in communication by telex with a Dutch company in Amsterdam. It was held that the contract was made in London, where the English company received the acceptance, even though the recipient did not read the telex until much later.
- However, in *Brinkibon v Stahag Stahl* (1983), a telex was received when the office was closed. It was held that the acceptance could become effective only when the office reopened.
- A problem may arise when both parties use their **own printed contract forms**. The Court of Appeal in *Butler Machine Tool v Ex-Cell-O Corporation* (1979) applied the principle that when there is a 'battle of forms', a contract is made when the last of the forms is sent and received without objection.

Typical mistake

Examiner reports indicate that candidates often overlook the fact that acceptance can be by conduct.

Key terms

Acceptance is unconditional and unqualified agreement to all the terms in the offer.

Exam tip

You may be asked a general question, for example one asking what acceptance is, or a more specific one, for example about the different ways in which acceptance can be communicated or about particular types of acceptance.

Almost certainly you will be asked to apply your understanding of offer/acceptance. Often this will involve looking at a sequence of events and deciding whether a contract has been made. It is a good idea to draw up a time line so that you identify exactly what happened at each stage. This should then enable you to work out whether a valid contract has been made or whether for example the offer was revoked before it was accepted.

Now test yourself 1

Tested ☐

1. Explain what a bilateral contract is.
2. Explain what a unilateral contract is.
3. Under what circumstances can a reward poster or reward advertisement become an offer? Which case confirms this?
4. Explain what is meant by the idea that an offer must be communicated.
5. What are the five ways in which an offer can be terminated?
6. What is an invitation to treat?
7. Which case confirms that goods on display in a supermarket are an invitation to treat?
8. What is the situation if conditions are attached to an acceptance?
9. Why was the 'acceptance' in *Felthouse v Bindley* not valid?
10. Explain what is meant by revocation of an offer.
11. What principle is set out in *Entores v Miles Far East*?
12. How will the courts deal with a situation where both parties use their own printed forms when making a contract?

Answers on p.137–138

Consideration

- Consideration means that each side must promise to give or do something for the other.
- It was defined in *Currie v Misa (1875)* as 'some right, interest, profit or benefit accruing to one party, or some forbearance, detriment, loss or responsibility given, suffered or undertaken by the other'.
- It is possible to have a valid contract even if one party does not provide consideration (e.g. if someone promises to make a gift), but only if the contract is made by deed.

Rules of consideration

- **Something of value must be given by both/all parties**. The law says that consideration must be sufficient – this means that it must have some actual value.
- **It does not have to be adequate** (i.e. the market price). Providing consideration has some value, the courts will not investigate its adequacy, nor will they investigate contracts to see if the parties have got equal value.
- In *Chappell and Co. Ltd v Nestlé Co. Ltd (1960)*, Nestlé was running a special offer which involved people sending off three wrappers from Nestlé chocolate bars plus some money. It was held that the three wrappers were part of the consideration, even though on receipt the wrappers were thrown away.
- **It must not be past**. This means that any consideration must come after the agreement, rather than being something that has already been done. For example, if A paints B's house and then when the work is finished B promises to pay £100 for the work, this promise is unenforceable because A's consideration is past.
- In *Re McArdle (1951)* repairs were made to a property and afterwards people who were to inherit the property were asked to sign an agreement that they would reimburse the cost of the repairs. This agreement was not enforceable because the repairs had been done before the agreement was made.
- **It must not be an existing duty**, i.e. doing something that you are already bound to do cannot amount to good consideration.
- In *Stilk v Myrick (1809)*, when two out of eleven sailors deserted a ship the captain promised to pay the remaining crew extra money if they sailed the ship back. But as the sailors were already bound by their contract to sail back and to meet such emergencies of the voyage, promising to sail back was not valid consideration.
- However, in *Hartley v Ponsonby (1857)*, when 19 out of 36 crew of a ship deserted, the captain promised to pay the remaining crew extra money to sail back, and it was held that sailing the ship back in such dangerous conditions was over and above their normal duties.
- *Williams v Roffey (1991)* seems to indicate that in business contracts the courts will try to find consideration in circumstances where, on the face of it, the consideration appears to be part of an existing duty.

> **Key terms**
>
> Consideration is the idea that each party to a contract must contribute something of value to it.

> **Exam tip**
>
> You may be asked a general question about what is meant by consideration, or a more specific question about what is meant by past consideration. You could also be asked to apply your understanding and decide whether good consideration has been offered in a particular scenario.

- **Third parties and consideration**: some contracts involve an agreement to benefit someone other than the parties to the agreement. This raises the principle of **privity of contract**, which is the idea that only people who are a party to a contract can enforce it, even though it might intend to benefit third parties.

- Modern law, as set out in the Contracts (Rights of Third Parties) Act 1999, has significantly altered the position of third parties, allowing them to enforce agreements where they are expressly identified as beneficiaries.

Intention to create legal relations
Revised ☐

- The law says that there must be an intention to create legal relations.

- It makes a distinction between **social** and **domestic agreements**, where the law assumes that there is no intention to create legal relations, and **commercial** and **business agreements**, where the law assumes that the parties intend the agreement to be legally binding.

Social and domestic agreements

- Agreements within families will generally be treated as not legally binding. For example, in *Jones v Padavatton (1969)*, Mrs Jones offered a monthly allowance to her daughter if she would give up her job in the USA and come to England, but there was no intention to create legal relations and all the arrangements were just part of ordinary family life.

> **Exam tip**
>
> An exam question may ask you to explain the meaning of 'intention to create legal relations' and it might ask you how this applies to the facts in the scenario.

- In *Balfour v Balfour (1919)* a promise was made by a husband to pay his wife an allowance while he was abroad. It was held that arrangements between husbands and wives are not contracts because the parties do not intend them to be legally binding.

- However, in *Merrit v Merrit (1970)* the husband left his wife and they made an agreement about future arrangements. When the agreement was made, the husband and wife were no longer living together, so they must have intended the agreement to be binding.

- In cases that do not just involve members of the same family, the presumption that the arrangement is purely social will be rebutted if money has changed hands.

- In *Parker v Clarke (1960)*, a young couple, the Parkers, were persuaded by an older couple to sell their house and move in with them. They would share the bills and the younger couple would inherit the house. Details of expenses were agreed and confirmation of the agreement was put in writing. It was held that the actions of the parties showed that they were serious and the agreement was intended to be legally binding.

Commercial and business agreements

- An agreement made in a business context is presumed to be legally binding unless a different intent can be shown. In *Rose v Crompton Bros (1925)* it was held that the sole agency agreement was not binding because there was a clause that it was not entered into as a formal or legal agreement.

- Football pools are a specific exception to the rule that agreements of a commercial nature are presumed to be legally binding. In *Jones v Vernon Pools (1938)* the courts ruled that a statement on the coupon that the transaction was 'binding in honour only' meant that it was not legally binding.

- On the other hand, situations where free gifts or prizes are promised are deemed to be legally binding, because the purpose is generally to promote the commercial interests of the body offering the gift or prize.

- In *McGowan v Radio Buxton (2001)*, a prize in a radio competition was stated to be a Renault Clio car. However, when the prize was awarded it was a model car rather than a real one. The court held that there was an intention to create legal relations and also that, looking at the transcript of the broadcast, people entering the competition would expect the prize to be a real car.

Now test yourself 2

Tested

1. Under what circumstances can there be a valid contract without consideration?
2. What principle about consideration was illustrated in *Chappell v Nestlé*?
3. Explain what past consideration is.
4. Why was the outcome in *Hartley v Ponsonby* different to that in *Stylk v Myrick*?
5. How was the position of third parties altered by the Contracts (Rights of Third Parties) Act 1999?
6. What rule of law does *Jones v Padavattan* illustrate?
7. Why were *Balfour v Balfour* and *Merrit v Merrit* decided differently?
8. What suggested that the agreement in *Parker v Clarke* was intended to be legally binding?
9. Why was the agreement not legally binding in *Rose v Crompton Bros*?
10. What type of agreement is a specific exception to the rule that agreements of a commercial nature should be legally binding?

Answers on p.138

Check your understanding

1 Complete the tables below.

Consideration rules	Case example	Facts of case that demonstrate rule
Must have value, but does not have to be adequate	Chappell and Co. Ltd v Nestlé Co. Ltd	
It must not be past	Re McArdle	
It must not be an existing duty	Stilk v Myrick	

Elements of formation of contract	Definition
Offer	
Invitation to treat	
Acceptance	
Consideration	

2 Match the cases with the facts and state the relevant area of law.

Case	Facts	Area of law
	Three chocolate bar wrappers	
	Letter lost in post	
	If I don't hear ……. the horse will be mine	
	Husband left wife and agreed to pay her income	
	Promise to help pay for improvements to house before agreement was made	
	Drugs on shelves in a chemist	
	Acceptance by telex	
	Flick knives in shop window	
	Advert to sell wild birds	
	Won model car	
	Letter revoking offer received after acceptance	
	Claimed reward of £100	
	W offered to sell farm for £1000. H said £950	

Re McArdle	Chappell and Co. Ltd v Nestlé Co. Ltd	Merritt v Merritt	McGowan v Buxton
Entores v Miles Far East	Hyde v Wrench	Household Fire Insurance v Grant	Felthouse v Bindley
Fisher v Bell	Byrne v van Tienhoven	Partridge v Crittenden	Pharmaceutical Soc. v Boots
Carlill v Carbolic Smoke Ball Co.			

Answers on p.138

Exam practice

James wanted his kitchen painted and he telephoned William, a painter and decorator, who had been recommended by a friend. William was not in so James left a message on his telephone answering machine asking when he would be available to do the work and mentioning that the friend had said that William had charged him £750. William sent a text saying 'I might be available next week.' James then sent a text saying 'OK, that's agreed, you will do it next week for £750.' The following day Ben tells James that he will do the work for £700 and can start straight away. James agrees, but Ben does not actually start until the next week and he says that it will take longer than he thought and will cost £800.

1 Outline the rules that apply to acceptance of an offer. **[8 marks]**

2 Discuss whether there is a contract between James and William. **[8 marks]**

Online

Exam summary

✔ You could be asked to explain the rules on offer and acceptance, including invitations to treat, the ending of offers and the different forms of acceptance, such as conduct/post.

✔ You may also be asked to apply these rules to a factual scenario and to decide the significance of the stages of negotiation and whether a contract has been made.

✔ You could be asked to explain consideration, including past consideration or intention to create legal relations. Along with offer and acceptance they are essential elements in the formation of contract. You may also have to apply them to a factual scenario and decide whether a contract exists.

14 Breach of contract and the courts: procedure and damages

For this topic you need to understand:

- what is meant by breach of contract and different types of breach
- remedies available to the injured party
- purposes of damages and how damages are calculated
- the procedure followed and the courts used if a case is taken to court
- burden and standard of proof in contract cases.

Breach of contract and different types of breach
Revised

- When a party fails to perform an obligation under a contract, it is said to be in breach of contract.
- **Actual breach** is when there is a failure to fulfil an obligation under the contract or to fulfil it to the required standard.
- **Anticipatory breach** occurs when one party shows by express words or by implications from his or her conduct at some time before performance is due that he or she does not intend to observe his or her obligations under the contract.
- In cases of anticipatory breach, the innocent party is not under any obligation to wait until the date fixed for performance but may immediately treat the contract as at an end and sue for damages.
- This principle was established in *Hochester v De La Tour (1853)*, where an employer told his employee (a travelling courier) before the time for performance arrived that he would not require his services. It was held that he could sue for damages at once.
- The injured party in an anticipatory breach of contract also has the option of waiting for the performance date to pass and then suing for breach.
- For example, in *Avery v Bowden (1855)*, a case involving an agreement to supply cargo for a ship at a port in Russia, the claimant waited the 45 days until the date the cargo was due to be supplied and then sued. Meanwhile, the Crimean War had broken out and performance of the contract became illegal.

> **Exam tip**
>
> Be prepared for a general question on what breach of contract is and also for a question asking you the difference between actual and anticipatory breach. You can also expect to have to apply your understanding to a specific scenario and explain whether someone is in breach of contract.

> **Key terms**
>
> Breach of contract is a failure by someone to perform their obligations under a contract.

Remedies available to the injured party
Revised

- **The rights of the injured party depend on the nature of the term broken.**
- A **breach of warranty** is a breach of a minor term that does not go to the root of the contract and only gives rise to a claim for damages.
- A **breach of a condition** is a breach of an important term, giving the right to terminate the agreement and repudiate (cancel) the contract.

- An example of breach of warranty is *Bettini v Gye (1876)* in which an opera singer missed the first two rehearsals. This was only a minor inconvenience, but in *Poussard v Spiers and Pond (1876)* an opera singer whose role was central missed the first six performances and this was a breach of condition.
- The injured party is prevented from using a minor breach of contract as an excuse for cancelling the whole contract.
- For example, if a new car is delivered that has a faulty interior light, it is reasonable to expect the supplier to put it right at the supplier's expense (damages), but not reasonable to allow the purchaser to cancel the contract and demand his or her money back. However, if there was a series of technical failures which were not easy to put right and which resulted in the car breaking down, these relate to the very purpose of the contract.

Repudiation of the contract

- Repudiation is available only when there has been a breach of a condition.
- It is a drastic remedy and will result in any goods supplied or money paid under the contract being returned.

Damages

- This remedy is available for all kinds of breach of contract, and may be appropriate even in cases where the contract has been rescinded.
- Damages may be classified as either liquidated or unliquidated.
- **Liquidated damages** are where the parties agree in advance what would be reasonable compensation in the event of a breach.
- **Unliquidated damages** are those which have not been agreed to in advance and they will be determined by the court.

Purpose of damages and how damages are calculated

Revised

- As stated in *Robinson v Harman (1848)*, the principle is that 'when a party sustains loss by reason of a breach of contract, he is, so far as money can do it, to be placed in the same situation with respect to damages as if the contract had been performed'.

Causation

- There must be a causal link between the breach of contract and the damage suffered. This is a question of fact in each case.
- If the loss arises partly from the breach and partly as a result of intervening events, the party in breach may still be liable, providing the chain of causation has not been broken.
- For example, in *Stansbie v Troman (1948)*, a decorator failed to lock the premises he had been working in and a thief entered and stole property. He was liable for the loss because it was the result of his failure to comply with his contractual duty to secure the premises on leaving.

Remoteness of damage

- The courts must decide how far the losses suffered by the injured party should be recoverable. The principle used is that losses are recoverable if they are reasonably within the contemplation of the parties as a probable result of the breach.
- This principle is known as the rule in *Hadley v Baxendale (1854)*. In that case, a new mill shaft was ordered and the carriers were late in

delivering it, with the result that the whole mill was out of action for several days. The carriers said that they had not been told that the existing shaft was broken and therefore they did not know that their delay would result in the mill being unable to function.

Exam tip

Although the wording of the question might vary, you are likely to be asked how the court would calculate the amount of damages to be awarded. In your answer you need to refer to all the elements in this section.

- It was held that they were not liable for the loss of profit and damages should be awarded only for losses that could fairly and reasonably be considered to have arisen naturally or those that may be supposed to have been in the contemplation of the parties at the time they made the contract.

- The principle was applied in *Victoria Laundry v Newman Industries (1949)*, in which a boiler was not delivered on time. Damages for the loss of profits from the laundry business were recoverable, but losses from not being able to take up a lucrative dyeing contract were not recoverable, because the defendant company had no knowledge of this contract and could not be expected to have had it in contemplation.

Mitigation of loss

- It is the duty of every party claiming damages to mitigate loss. This means that they need to ensure that as far as possible losses are kept to a minimum.

- The claimant cannot recover for loss that could have been avoided by taking reasonable steps.

- The claimant cannot recover for any loss that has actually been avoided, even if the claimant went further than was necessary in compliance with the above rule.

- The claimant may recover loss incurred in taking reasonable steps unsuccessfully to mitigate loss.

- In *British Westinghouse v Underground Electric Railway of London (1912)*, there was a contract for the supply of turbines, but those supplied were not efficient and the buyer replaced them with turbines that were more efficient than those specified in the original contract. It was held that the financial advantages gained from the new turbines had to be taken into account.

Key terms

Mitigation is the idea that the injured party should do what they reasonably can to reduce the losses resulting from the breach of contract.

- However, a claimant is only expected to do what is reasonable. For example, in *Pilkington v Wood (1953)*, the claimant bought a house with defective title because of his solicitor's negligence. He did not have to mitigate his loss by suing the vendor.

Now test yourself 1   Tested ☐

1 What is 'anticipatory breach'?
2 What are the two options open to the victim of anticipatory breach?
3 What additional right is available for a breach of condition that is not available for a breach of warranty?
4 What is the purpose of damages?
5 What is the principle used to decide if losses from a breach of contract should be recoverable?
6 In which case was this principle set out?
7 What losses were not recoverable in *Victoria Laundry v Newman Industries*?
8 What is meant by the requirement that claimants should mitigate their loss?
9 What was the mitigation that reduced the losses in *British Westinghouse v Underground Electric Railway of London*?
10 What principle was established by *Pilkington v Wood*?

Answers on p.139

The courts and procedure in contract cases

Revised

- The two Civil Courts in which a contract claim might be brought are the County Court and the High Court.

Starting a civil action

- Most simple contract claims will start in the County Court. Money Claim Online allows claims for fixed sums up to £100,000 to be issued online in the County Court. But complex cases over £25,000 can be heard in the High Court (Queen's Bench Division).

- The person who starts the action is called the claimant and they issue a Claim Form. There is a court fee which increases with the size of claim. In 2007 the minimum was £30, up to a maximum of £1700 (for claims over £300,000). The person who is sued by the claimant is called the defendant.

> **Key terms**
>
> The claimant is the person who brings an action in a civil court and the defendant is the person against whom the action is brought.

Options for the defendant

- When the Claim Form is served on the defendant (i.e. when they receive it), they have a number of options:
  - Admit the claim and pay the money.
  - Defend the claim – if they do this they must serve a defence.
  - If the defendant does nothing then after 14 days the claimant can apply for a default judgment – the defendant will have to pay the full amount.

The tracks

Revised

- The three tracks that a contract case could be allocated to are the small claims, fast track and multi-track.

Small claims track

- For claims up to £10,000. There is a flexible informal procedure and no orders for costs, to encourage people to represent themselves.

Fast track

- For straightforward cases from £10,000 to £25,000. In practice, all Money Claims Online cases would be dealt with under this procedure. There will be a preliminary hearing to lay down a timetable. Cases are put on a strict timetable and must be heard in 30 weeks.

Multi-track

- For claims over £25,000 or for complex cases below that amount.
- In the County Court they are heard by a Circuit judge who will manage the case to speed it up and save costs.
- All cases over £50,000, other than those started under Money Claims Online, have to be heard in the High Court, and some complex cases over £25,000 will be heard there.
- The multi-track is the only track used in the High Court.
- There will be a case management hearing where the judge will impose a timetable for procedural issues to be resolved.

> **Typical mistake**
>
> Students use the old limits for the tracks – the mark schemes states that these are not creditworthy.

Alternative dispute resolution

Revised

- The vast majority of cases are settled and do not go to court.
- Of those that go to court, most are settled before coming to trial.

- People are encouraged to use other forms of civil dispute resolution.
- If one of the parties unreasonably refuses to consider this option, the court has the power to disallow legal costs, as happened in *Dunnett v Railtrack*.
- The types of alternative dispute resolution available are:
  - negotiation – the parties try and reach agreement together
  - mediation – a go-between will help the parties reach agreement
  - conciliation – a go-between will offer advice or a solution, which the parties can accept or reject.

Key terms

Other forms of civil dispute resolution mean using informal methods like negotiation, mediation or conciliation to settle a dispute. These methods can be used as an alternative to going to court or at any stage during the court process.

Burden and standard of proof

Revised

- In most civil cases, the burden of proof is on the claimant to prove his or her case against the defendant.
- The standard of proof is '**on the balance of probabilities**' – a lower standard than in criminal cases.

Now test yourself 2

Tested

1 What are the options that the defendant has when they are served with a Claim Form?
2 What are the three tracks that a civil case for breach of contract could be allocated to?
3 What are the financial limits for each track?
4 Which is the only track used in the High Court?
5 What are the three other forms of civil dispute resolution open to the parties to use?
6 What is the standard of proof in civil cases?

Answers on p.139

Check your understanding

1 Match the cases with the facts and areas of law

Case	Facts	Area of law
	Man was hired as courier	
	Turbines did not match specifications	
	Decorator given keys of house	
	New boiler needed for dyeing contract	
	An opera singer missed the first two rehearsals	
	An opera singer whose role was central missed the first six performances	

Hochster v de la Tour	*Stansbie v Troman*	*Victoria Laundry v Newman Industries*
Westinghouse v Underground Electric Railways	*Bettini v Gye*	*Poussard v Spiers and Pond*

2 Complete the table to show how damages are calculated.

Stages	Explanation of rule	Case which confirms rule
1 The purpose of damages		
2 Causation		
3 Remoteness		
4 Mitigation		

Answers on p.139

Exam practice

James wanted his kitchen painted and he telephoned William, a painter and decorator, who had been recommended by a friend. William was not in so James left a message on his telephone answering machine asking when he would be available to do the work and mentioning that the friend had said that William had charged him £750. William sent a text saying 'I might be available next week. ' James then sent a text saying 'OK, that's agreed, you will do it next week for £750.' The following day Ben tells James that he will do the work for £700 and can start straight away. James agrees, but Ben does not actually start until the next week and he says that it will take longer than he thought and will cost £800.

1 Explain what is meant by breach of contract and assuming that there is a contract between James and Ben, discuss whether Ben is in breach of that contract.   **[8 marks]**

2 Explain how the court will calculate any damages that might be payable by Ben to James.   **[8 marks]**

Online

Exam summary

✔ You could be asked to explain breach of contract, including actual and anticipatory breach. You may also have to apply these rules to a factual scenario.

✔ There is often a question of calculation of damages. Make sure you refer to the purpose of damages and the rule in *Hadley v Baxendale*. You may have to apply the rules to a factual scenario.

✔ You are likely to be asked a question on the procedure followed in a contract case or on the courts/tracks which would be used in the situation in the scenario. You may also be asked about opportunities for settling out of court.

Unit 1 Answers

1: Parliamentary law making

Now test yourself 1

1 It sets out its proposals for new legislation.

2 Pressure groups that have direct contact with government ministers and Parliament.

3 Civil Partnership Act 2004

4 Trade unions, National Farmers' Union (NFU) or British Medical Association.

5 Television, radio, newspapers and journals.

6 The publication in 2009 of MP's expenses claims by the *Daily Telegraph*.

7 Dangerous Dogs Act 1991

8 1965

9 Looking at reform of the law, codification and consolidation.

10 Reform of non-fatal offences.

Now test yourself 2

1 A consultative document setting out ideas for legislation.

2 Abortion Act 1967

3 Second reading

4 Parliament Acts 1911 and 1949

5 Access to Justice Act 1999

6 1707

7 Northern Ireland Act 1972

8 The idea that as a democratically elected body – Parliament – is the supreme law-making body in the country.

9 No Parliament can make laws that will restrict law making in future Parliaments.

10 *A and others v Sec of State for Home Dept (2004)*

Check your understanding

1 In the table below briefly explain two advantages and two disadvantages of each influence on Parliament.

Advantages of Law Commission	Responsible for many sensible changes to the law, for example the abolition of the 'Year and a day' rule.
	Produces draft Bills ready for Parliament to introduce, which reduces the workload for ministers.
Disadvantages of Law Commission	Parliament has often ignored the Commission's proposals, e.g. the proposals on reform of non-fatal offences have never been implemented.
	Law Commission investigates as many as 20–30 areas at the same time. This may mean that each investigation is not very thorough.

Advantages of pressure groups	Pressure groups give the public and particularly minorities a voice. They act as a safety valve for frustrations, as in pro-hunting and anti-Iraq War protests.
	They raise public awareness of issues that affect their interest or cause, e.g. through a variety of stunts, Fathers 4 Justice has been successful in raising awareness of the plight of many fathers denied access to their children after a divorce.
Disadvantages of pressure groups	It is difficult for smaller pressure groups to match the influence of larger ones. Environmental groups claim that the strength of the road lobby and the airline industry means that new roads or airport extensions are difficult to fight.
	Pressure groups may only represent a minority view when they are successful in changing the law, as was arguably the case when the death penalty was abolished in 1966.
Advantages of the media	The media play a powerful role in bringing issues to the attention of Parliament or the Government and can force it to act. An example is the publication in 2009 of MP's expenses claims by the *Daily Telegraph*.
	Coverage in newspapers and on television and radio can raise the public profile of an issue and add weight to public opinion.
Disadvantages of the media	Ownership of British newspapers and other branches of the media is in the hands of a relatively small number of individuals, e.g. Rupert Murdoch.
	The media may sometimes whip up public opinion which may result in unwise legislation, as was arguably the case with the Dangerous Dogs Act 1991.

2 For a Bill starting in the House of Commons briefly summarise in the table below what happens at each stage.

First reading	The title of the Bill is read out to the House.
Second reading	The House holds a full debate on the main principles of the Bill. At the end of the debate, a vote is taken as to whether the Bill should proceed further.
Committee stage	This involves a detailed examination of each clause of the Bill by a standing committee of between 16 and 50 MPs.
Report stage	The committee reports back to the House on any amendments that have been made. These are debated and voted on.
Third reading	The Bill is presented again to the House and the final vote is taken.
House of Lords	The same procedure is repeated. If the House of Lords make amendments to a Bill that has already passed through the House of Commons, the Bill is referred back to the Commons to consider the amendments.
Royal Assent	The Bill receives the formal consent of the monarch in order to become law.

2: Delegated legislation

Now test yourself 1

1 It is an Act that delegates power to others to make more detailed law.

2 Local Government Act 1972 or Access to Justice Act 1999

3 The Queen and Privy Council

4 The Traffic Signs Regulations 2002 which regulate the size and colour of road signs.

5 The relevant government minister.

6 A vote in Parliament approving it.

7 It reviews all statutory instruments and can draw the attention of Parliament to any that need special consideration.

8 It is where a public authority has not followed the procedures set out in the enabling Act for creating delegated legislation.

9 *AG v Fulham Corporation (1921)*

10 Air Navigation Order 1995

11 During the Foot and Mouth crisis of 2001.

12 It is where the Statutory Instrument is made by civil servants in the relevant government departments rather than by the ministers who were originally given the delegated powers.

Check your understanding

1 Fill in the missing information on controls by Parliament and controls by the Judiciary.

Controls by Parliament
Parliament can set LIMITS in the ENABLING ACT.
There are two COMMITTEES. The first is THE DELEGATED POWERS SCRUTINY COMMITTEE IN THE HOUSE OF LORDS.
The second is THE JOINT COMMITTEE ON STATUTORY INSTRUMENTS.
AFFIRMATIVE RESOLUTION. This is where DELEGATED LEGISLATION HAS TO BE LAID BEFORE BOTH HOUSES, AND IT ONLY BECOMES LAW IF A VOTE TO APPROVE IT IS TAKEN WITHIN A SPECIFIED TIME.
Example: UNDER THE HUNTING ACT 2004, THE MINISTER MAY ALLOW HUNTING WITH DOGS IN SOME CIRCUMSTANCES AS LONG AS PARLIAMENT CONSENTS.
NEGATIVE RESOLUTION. This is where THE DELEGATED LEGISLATION IS PUT BEFORE PARLIAMENT AND IF NO MEMBER HAS PUT DOWN A MOTION TO ANNUL IT WITHIN A SPECIFIED PERIOD (USUALLY 40 DAYS) IT BECOMES LAW.
It is used for most STATUTORY INSTRUMENTS.
Parliament can REPEAL the ENABLING ACT.

Controls by the Judiciary
An action can be brought for JUDICIAL REVIEW in the HIGH COURT and the court can decide that the DL is *ULTRA VIRES*. This means that the body making it has gone BEYOND its POWERS.
SUBSTANTIVE *ULTRA VIRES*. This is where the body making the DL did not have the AUTHORITY in the ENABLING ACT for doing this.
An example is *AG V FULHAM CORPORATION*.
PROCEDURAL *ULTRA VIRES*. This is where the body making the DL has not FOLLOWED THE PROCEDURES SET OUT IN THE ENABLING ACT.
An example is *AGRICULTURAL, HORTICULTURAL AND FORESTRY TRAINING BOARD V AYLESBURY MUSHROOMS LTD*.
The courts might decide that a piece of DL is UNREASONABLE.
An example is *STRICKLAND V HAYES*.

2 Develop each of the points in the table below, explaining why each is a reason for having delegated legislation.

Saves Parliament's time	There is not enough time for Parliament to consider every detail of every regulation/ rule. Delegated legislation frees Parliament to concentrate on broad issues of policy rather than masses of detail.	
Technical expertise	Parliament does not have the knowledge or technical expertise necessary in certain areas, such as building regulations or health and safety regulations at work. Delegating legislation allows the use of experts in the relevant areas to make the rule.	
Local needs	Local people know local needs. For example, Cornwall County Council are the best people to make rules for libraries in Cornwall.	
Speed	It can be made more quickly than an Act of Parliament. Orders in Council can be used in emergencies when Parliament is not sitting.	
Easily revoked	An Act of Parliament requires another statute to amend or revoke it, which takes much longer.	

3: Statutory interpretation

Now test yourself 1

1 Things inside the Act, which can help with interpretation.
2 *R v Tivnan (1999)*
3 Section 10 of the Theft Act 1968
4 Things outside the Act which may help with interpretation.
5 *Cheeseman* or *Vaughan v Vaughan*
6 *Pepper v Hart*
7 *Ejusdem generis*
8 Express mention of one thing implies the exclusion of another.

Now test yourself 2

1 Giving words their plain, ordinary, dictionary meaning.
2 Because her husband was maintaining and not relaying or repairing the track.
3 Michael Zander
4 *R v Allen*
5 *Adler v George*
6 A murderer inheriting from his victim.
7 *Heydon's Case (1584)*
8 Illegal, 'backstreet' abortions
9 Lord Denning
10 *Pepper v Hart*
11 *Jones v Tower Boot Co* or *R v Registrar General ex parte Smith*
12 *R v Deegan*

Check your understanding

1 Identify the case and the rule the case illustrates.

Facts	Case	Rule
maintaining not repairing	Berriman's case	Literal
in the vicinity of	*Adler v George*	Golden
in the street	*Smith v Hughes*	Mischief
being married shall marry again	Allen	Golden
downloaded pornography	Porter	Literal
someone entitled to vote	*Whiteley v Chappell*	Literal
posed a risk to his mother	AG v Reg Gen ex parte Smith	Purposive
you can refer to Hansard	*Pepper v Hart*	Purposive
a registered medical practitioner	RCN v DHSS	Mischief
racial harassment in the course of employment	*Jones v Tower Boot*	Purposive

4: Judicial precedent

Now test yourself 1

1 The principle that higher courts bind lower courts.
2 Depart from its own earlier decisions.
3 *Young v Bristol Aeroplane Co*
4 The reasons for deciding – the part of the judgment where the reasons for the decision are set out.

5 To be reckless you have to know there is a risk of an unlawful consequence and decide to take the risk.
6 Precedent that judges in future cases may choose to follow, but they are not bound to.
7 Other things said, i.e. comments by the judge that are not directly related to the decision in the case.
8 *R v Gotts*
9 *Hedley Byrne v Heller* followed the dissenting judgment in *Candler Crane v Christmas*.
10 Attorney General for *Jersey v Holley*
11 1865
12 Those produced by the Incorporated Council of Law Reporting (ICLR).

Now test yourself 2

1 It is where the facts of a case are sufficiently different to those in the case setting the precedent to enable a judge to not follow the precedent.
2 *Merritt v Merritt* was distinguished from *Balfour v Balfour* or *Wilson* was distinguished from *Brown*.
3 It is where a Judge states that they think an earlier precedent was wrongly decided, but are obliged to follow it because of precedent. The disapproval may influence decisions in later cases.
4 It allows people to know what the law is, enabling lawyers to predict the likely outcome of a case.
5 *R v R*
6 Because judges can only make law on the facts of the case before them. They cannot lay down a comprehensive code to cover all possible situations.
7 Because the strict hierarchy means that judges have to follow binding precedent. Therefore, bad or inappropriate decisions cannot be changed unless they are heard in a higher court that can overrule them.
8 Applying to events that occurred before the case was brought.

Check your understanding

1 Choose a case to illustrate each of the following elements of precedent.

Element of precedent	Case
Supreme Court Practice Statement	*British Railways Board v Herrington (1972)* – overruled *Addie v Dumbreck (1929)*
Court of Appeal (Civil Division)	*Young v Bristol Aeroplane Co Ltd (1944)*
Court of Appeal (Criminal Division)	*R v Simpson (2003)*
Ratio decidendi	the rule in *R v Nedrick (1986)*
Obiter dicta	*obiter* statement in *R v Howe (1987)* that duress was not available to a charge of attempted murder was followed in *R v Gotts (1992)*
Persuasive from lower court	House of Lords agreed with the reasons that the Court of Appeal gave in the case of *R v R (1991)*

Element of precedent	Case
Persuasive from dissenting judgment	Dissenting judgment in *Candler v Crane Christmas (1951)* was followed by the House of Lords in *Hedley Byrne v Heller (1964)*
Persuasive from Privy Council	*Attorney General for Jersey v Holley (2005)*
Persuasive from foreign court	*Caparo v Dickman (1990)* approved a statement in an Australian case
Distinguishing	*Merritt v Merritt (1970)* distinguished from *Balfour v Balfour (1919)*

2   Complete the tables by adding a comment explaining the advantages and disadvantages of precedent.

Advantages	
Certainty	Allows people to know what the law is, enabling lawyers to predict the likely outcome of a case. Lord Reid in *Knuller v DPP* said 'in the interests of certainty', there had to be a good reason for changing a precedent.
Flexibility	Allows the law to evolve. Changes in attitude in society can be taken into account, an example being *R v R (1991)*, when the House of Lords accepted that a man could be guilty of raping his wife.
Real life situations	The law develops in a very practical, common sense way because it is dealing with real cases. This is better than having Parliament legislate in a theoretical way.

Disadvantages	
Large number of cases	This makes it difficult to know all the cases that might be relevant. Judges may only be aware of those precedents that the parties concerned bring to their attention.
Rigid	The strict hierarchy means that judges have to follow binding precedent. Therefore, bad or inappropriate decisions cannot be changed unless they are heard in a higher court that can overrule them.
Unsystematic	Judges can only make law on the facts of the case before them. They cannot lay down a comprehensive code to cover all possible situations, as Parliament can.
Illogical distinctions	There may be only minute and apparently illogical differences between some cases. Too many distinctions of this type can lead to unpredictability.
Undemocratic	Judges are actually making law, which under the doctrine of the separation of powers is not part of their role.
Retrospective	Precedent refers back to events that occurred before the case was brought. This could lead to unfairness if, as a result of the case, the law is changed, because the parties to the case could not have known what the law was prior to their actions. This is what happened in *R v R (1991)*.

5: The Civil Courts and other forms of dispute resolution

Now test yourself 1

1   County Court and High Court

2   Small claims; fast track; multi-track

3   Court of Appeal (Civil Division), with the possibility of a further appeal to the Supreme Court on an issue of law of public importance.

4   Tribunals, Courts and Enforcement Act 2007

5   Cases are decided by a judge and two lay people with relevant expertise (the panel).

6   To hear appeals.

7   Employment tribunal

8   These are 'in house' tribunals set up by professional bodies.

Now test yourself 2

1   Arbitration is where both parties voluntarily agree to an independent third party making a decision in their case.

2   Arbitration Act 1996

3   Commercial arbitration and consumer arbitration.

4   An Award

5   The conciliator plays an active part and offers non-binding suggestions and advice.

6   Mediation

7   Negotiation

8   The two parties talking to each other without a third party.

Now test yourself 3

1   One from the following: compulsory process; fair process supervised by experts; appeal process; legal aid; enforcement of decision.

2   It encourages tactical manoeuvring rather than cooperation.

3   The parties themselves choose the arbitrator, the procedure to be adopted, the time and place and the length of arbitration. They can also agree to limit the arbitrator's powers.

4   Only if there was a 'serious irregularity' in the proceedings.

5   West Kent Mediation

6   They are based on compromise so that the parties are less likely to feel embittered by the outcome.

7   Because these forms of civil dispute resolution are informal and based on compromise it can allow a wealthier party or one that is in a stronger bargaining position to force an unfavourable settlement on the weaker party.

8   An argument between neighbours over a tiny strip of land actually went to court.

Check your understanding

1   Fill in the table below which gives a summary of the Civil Courts process.

Size of claim	Court/track	Appeals
Up to £1000 personal injury claim	County/small claims	To a Circuit judge in the County Court. Further appeal to the Court of Appeal (Civil Division) in exceptional cases
Up to £10,000 other claims	County/small claims	To a Circuit judge in the County Court. Further appeal to the Court of Appeal (Civil Division) in exceptional cases
£10,000–£25,000	County/fast track	To a High Court judge in the High Court. Further appeal to Court of Appeal (Civil Division) in exceptional cases
Over £25,000	County or high/multi-track	To the Court of Appeal (Civil Division). Further appeal to Supreme Court if point of law of general public importance

2 Fill in the table below which gives a summary table of the types of civil dispute resolution.

Arbitration characteristics and examples	Binding award made by third party. Examples: Commercial arbitrations and consumer arbitrations.
Two advantages	Proceedings are held in private, an important consideration for commercial disputes. Parties retain more control over arbitration than over a court case.
Two disadvantages	The arbitrator is unlikely to have the same legal knowledge as a judge and this may result in a decision which ignores important legal points, especially if they are complex and technical. The parties can only appeal if there was a 'serious irregularity' in the proceedings.
Conciliation characteristics and examples	Third party helps parties reach agreement. May suggest non-binding solution. Examples: ACAS offers a conciliation scheme in industrial disputes. The British Vehicle Renting and Leasing Association (BVRLA) helps to solve disputes between car hire companies and people who hire cars.
Mediation characteristics and examples	Third party acts as a go-between to facilitate cooperation and agreement. Non-binding solution. Examples: Commercial mediation is promoted and organised by companies such as International Resolution Europe Ltd and the Centre for Dispute Resolution. Mediation in family disputes is available from the National Association of Family Mediation and Conciliation Services.

Negotiation characteristics and examples	Most basic and informal method. Parties communicate directly with each other. Examples: Low key disputes for example between a householder and a tradesman like an electrician or plumber or between neighbours. Bankruptcy Advisory Service takes the side of a bankrupt client and argues their case with the Official Receiver.
Two advantages of conciliation/ mediation/ negotiation	These methods are likely to be cheaper than using a court or tribunal because lawyers will probably not be needed. Negotiation, mediation and conciliation are based on compromise so that the parties are less likely to feel embittered by the outcome.
Two disadvantages of conciliation/ mediation/ negotiation	Often one party might be unwilling to compromise or feel angry and hostile to the other party. This makes it very difficult to use these methods. Because these forms of civil dispute resolution are informal and based on compromise it can allow a wealthier party or one that is in a stronger bargaining position to force an unfavourable settlement on the weaker party.

6: The criminal courts and lay people

Now test yourself 1

1 Magistrates' court

2 The magistrates have to decide whether they have jurisdiction, and if they have, the defendant then chooses the court.

3 Court of Appeal (Criminal Division) with the possibility of a further appeal to the Supreme Court if there is a point of law of public importance.

4 Aged between 18 and 65 and they are expected to live or work within or near the local justice area to which they are allocated.

5 The Lord Chancellor on the advice of county local advisory committees.

6 Two

7 Age, gender, ethnic background and occupation.

8 Judicial Studies Board

9 Competencies – the skills that magistrates need to develop.

10 Six months for a single offence or 12 months for multiple offences.

11 Two magistrates sit with a Circuit judge to hear appeals in the Crown Court.

12 They must have received additional training and there must be a mixed gender bench.

Now test yourself 2

1 Juries Act 1974 as amended by the Criminal Justice Act 1988

2 Those suffering from a mental illness and who are resident in a hospital or have regular treatment by a medical practitioner.

3 If their commanding officer certifies that their absence from duty would be prejudicial to the efficiency of the service.

4 The jury summoning officer.

5 In exceptional cases, such as those involving terrorism, the Official Secrets Acts and 'professional' criminals.

6 Determining guilt

7 Criminal Justice Act 1967

8 *Paul v DPP (1989)*

9 Approximately two-thirds have professional or managerial backgrounds and only about 4 per cent are under 40, while the great majority of defendants are young and from lower socio-economic groups.

10 *R v Ponting (1985)*, *R v Kronlid (1996)* or *R v Owen (1992)*

11 *R v Twomey*

12 *R v Young*

Check your understanding

1 Complete the table below.

Type of offence	Example of crime	Courts	Appeals
Summary	Assault	Magistrates'	Crown Court against conviction and/or sentence Point of law to the Divisional Court
Either way	Theft	Magistrates' or Crown	If tried by Magistrates – as for summary If tried in Crown Court – as for indictable
Indictable	Murder	Crown	Court of Appeal (Criminal Division) From the Court of Appeal to the Supreme Court if issue of law of public importance

2 Complete the table below to show the qualifications, selection and training of lay magistrates.

Qualifications	Aged between 18 and 65 and under the Courts Act 2003 they are expected to live or work within or near the local justice area to which they are allocated.
Selection and appointment	Appointed by the Lord Chancellor on the advice of county local advisory committees. Two interviews. Potential appointees are reviewed by the local advisory committee to ensure that a 'balanced bench' can be achieved in terms of age, gender, ethnic background and occupation.
Training	Organised by the Judicial Studies Board. Initial training is an intensive induction course. Core training in the first year and consolidation training at the end of the first year. Assessed for competencies. Extra training for chairs and youth and family panels.

3 Complete the tables below by adding some detail and discussion of the advantages and disadvantages of juries.

Advantages of juries	
Public participation	Juries allow the ordinary citizen to take part in the administration of justice, so that verdicts are seen to be those of society rather than of the judicial system.
Layman's equity	Act as a check on officialdom and protect against unjust or oppressive prosecution by reflecting a community's sense of justice e.g. *R v Ponting*.
Better decision making	Most cases come down to essential points of identification or witness credibility. These points are more likely to be decided correctly as a result of discussion between 12 unbiased and legally unqualified people than by a single judge.
Independence	Decisions made by juries have to be made without any outside influence.

Disadvantages of juries	
Lack of competence	Because of inexperience or ignorance jurors may rely too heavily on what they are told by lawyers at the expense of the real issues.
Jury nobbling	This is an attempt made by means of threats or bribery to 'persuade' a juror to return a 'not-guilty' verdict. In 1982, several Old Bailey trials had to be stopped because of attempted nobbling.
Cost and efficiency	Jury trials in the Crown Court are more expensive than trials in the Magistrates' Court. The cost of lawyers, judges and other court personnel will be higher and the case will last longer because of the need to sum up the evidence for the jury.
May decide unfairly	Jurors do not have to give reasoned verdicts and this, together with the fact that jury deliberations are secret, can lead to the suspicion that some jurors may not decide on the evidence in the case alone, e.g. *R v Young*.

7: The legal profession and other sources of advice and funding

Now test yourself 1

1 A 20-day professional skills course.

2 County and Magistrates' Courts

3 Dealing with the legal requirements of buying and selling property.

4 Gray's Inn, Lincoln's Inn, Inner Temple and Middle Temple.

5 Appear in court in minor cases by themselves.

6 This means that members of the public usually consult a solicitor first, who will then instruct a barrister if it is considered necessary.

7 Barristers have to accept any case referred to them, provided it lies within their legal expertise, the appropriate fee has been agreed and they are available at the time to accept the brief.

8 Specialist advice barristers provide to solicitors.

9 Approximately 10 per cent of barristers are QCs.

10 The minimum academic qualification is four GCSEs including English Language.

11 They are legal experts who collectively have experience in all aspects of legal work.

12 Cost

Now test yourself 2

1 Any two from: solicitors/barristers; CABs; Law Centres; insurance; trade unions/professional associations.

2 They specialise in housing, welfare or debt problems.

3 Community Legal Service

4 They allow cases to be brought by many people who would not have been eligible for legal aid.

5 Criminal Defence Service

6 Legal advice for suspects detained in police stations.

7 An assessment of someone's income and capital.

8 Interests of justice test

Check your understanding

1 Complete the tables below on the legal profession.

Solicitors	
Qualification	Law degree or other degree + GDL or CPE then LPC followed by two-year training contract. Entered on rolls of Law Society.
Work	Legal advice and carrying out administrative tasks, e.g. conveyancing, probate; drawing up contracts; setting up companies. Can act as advocates in Magistrates' and County Courts, in which they have 'rights of audience'. Can become solicitor advocates and have rights of audience in higher courts. Do preliminary work in all litigation. Usually work in partnerships. Increasingly solicitors will specialise in certain kinds of work.

Barristers	
Qualification	Law degree or other degree + GDL or CPE Member of Inns of Court, Bar Professional Course, 12 dinners. Called to Bar. One-year pupillage, secure tenancy.
Work	'Referral profession', but can now be engaged directly by certain professions and CABs and since 2004 Direct Public Access in civil law. 'Cab rank' rule. Most work is advocacy – rights of audience in all courts. Other main work is advice and drafting documents. Self-employed, work from chambers. About 10 per cent become QCs.

2 Complete the table below on advice and funding.

Area of law	Sources of advice	Sources of funding
Civil	Solicitors, CABs, Law Centres, private legal insurance, trade unions, professional bodies	State funding, CFAs, private funding
Criminal	Solicitors and barristers, duty solicitor scheme	State funding – duty solicitor advice and representation, criminal legal aid – means and interests of justice test. Private funding

8: The judiciary

Now test yourself 1

1 Five years' qualification as a solicitor or barrister.

2 Fifteen years' qualification as a solicitor or barrister or at least two years holding high judicial office.

3 The Judicial Appointments Commission (JAC).

4 From the ranks of High Court judges.

5 Because the Supreme Court is a court of the UK, not merely of England and Wales, by convention, two members are from Scotland and one from Northern Ireland.

6 Judicial Studies Board

7 Four days

8 Judicial College

Now test yourself 2

1 High Court judges

2 70

3 How much to award in damages if the claimant is successful, or what other remedy to grant; costs.

4 Summarise the evidence for the jury and direct it on relevant legal rules.

5 If a substantive critical motion is passed by both Houses of Parliament.

6 Inferior judges such as Circuit judges or District Court judges may be dismissed by the Lord Chief Justice acting together with the Lord Chancellor.

7 Office for Judicial Complaints

8 Montesquieu with his theory of the 'separation of powers'.

9 Tenure of office, judicial immunity from suit and immunity from parliamentary criticism.

10 The growing number of judicial review cases.

Check your understanding

1 Complete the table below on the role of judges.

Role of judges in civil cases	Allocating to appropriate track, dealing with pre-trial issues such as discovery of documents and agreeing a timetable. Preside over the court, decide legal issues. Decide case and award damages/costs.
Role of judges in criminal cases	Responsible for all matters of law and ensures rules of procedure are properly applied. Pre-trial issues – bail and legal aid. Maintains order, decides legal issues. Summarises the evidence for the jury and directs it on relevant legal rules. Sentences if defendant guilty.

2 Complete the table below on judicial independence.

Meaning	Free from any pressure from the government in particular, or from any political or other pressure groups so that those who appear before them and the wider public can have confidence that their cases will be decided fairly and in accordance with the law.
How secured	Tenure – all superior judges hold office 'during good behaviour', subject to removal only by the monarch by means of an address presented by both Houses of Parliament. No judge may be sued in respect of anything done while acting in his or her judicial capacity. No criticism of an individual judge may be made in either House of Parliament.
Evaluation	Because of an increase in judicial review cases, the responsibility of the judiciary to protect citizens against unlawful acts of government has increased, and with it the need for the judiciary to be independent of government. Importance is demonstrated in the many instances where judges have overruled the decisions of government ministers e.g. *A and others v Home Office*. It is particularly necessary when judges have to chair inquiries into major cases and national events e.g. Leveson Inquiry.

Unit 2 Answers

Chapter 9: Underlying principles of criminal liability

Now test yourself 1

1 A voluntary act is one in which the mind is in control of the body.

2 *Hill v Baxter*

3 A state of affairs is where the *actus reus* is the circumstances or condition of a person rather than in any act or omission on their part.

4 An example is *R v Winzar or Larsonneur*.

5 An omission is a failure to act.

6 The usual rule is that an omission cannot form the basis of *actus reus*.

7 Two exceptions are where it is a contractual duty to act e.g. *Pittwood* and where you fail to put right a dangerous condition you have created e.g. *Miller*. Other exceptions could be used.

8 Because she died of an entirely separate cause – a heart attack.

9 Legal causation

10 Because it was foreseeable that if he opened fire on the police they would fire back and kill the girl.

11 *Roberts* or *Halliday*.

12 It is the rule that if the victim suffers a pre-existing weakness or medical condition makes the consequence more serious for the victim than it would have been for other people you must take your victim as you find him and are therefore liable for all the consequences.

Now test yourself 2

1 Intention is where you act deliberately or make something your aim and purpose.

2 Oblique intent is where you know something is a virtually certain consequence of your action and yet you continue with the action.

3 *Matthews and Alleyne*. Could also have *Nedrick* or *Woollin* or *Hancock and Shankland*.

4   Recklessness is where you know there is a risk of a consequence and yet continue with the action.

5   *Cunningham* and *R v G* and others.

6   Transferred malice

7   The principle that there was really a series of acts which meant that if *mens rea* or *actus reus* applied at any stage in the series they applied to the whole series.

8   These are crimes that do not require any *mens rea*. Guilt is determined purely on the basis of *actus reus*.

9   *Callow v Tillstone* or *Harrow v Shah* or *Alphacell v Woodward*.

10 Those that are 'truly criminal'.

11 Help protect society by promoting greater care; offences are easier to enforce; saves court time as people are more likely to plead guilty.

12 Makes people guilty who are not blameworthy; even those who have taken all possible care will be found guilty and can be punished.

Now test yourself 3

1   Causing the victim to apprehend immediate unlawful personal violence.

2   *Constanza* or *Ireland*

3   *Logdon* or *Smith v Superintendent of Woking Police*

4   *Wilson v Pringle*

5   *Haystead v Chief Constable of Derbyshire* or *DPP v K* (a minor).

6   'Any hurt or injury calculated to interfere with the health or comfort of the victim provided it is not merely transient or trifling.'

7   *Savage* or *Roberts*

8   *C (a minor) v Eisenhower*

9   Intention or recklessness as to causing some harm, albeit not serious harm.

10 Any three of the following: fractured arm or leg, dislocated shoulder, permanent scarring, serious blood loss, serious psychiatric injury.

Check your understanding

1   Match the cases shown below the table with the facts and identify the relevant area of law.

Case	Facts	Area of law
Harrow v Shah	Newsagent and lottery ticket	Strict liability
Pittwood	Did not close gate	*Actus reus* – omissions
Woollin	Aimed to get baby into pram	*Mens rea* – oblique intent
White	Tried to poison mother	Causation – factual causation
Latimer	Aimed to hit man but hit woman	Transferred malice
Cunningham	Did not know there was a risk	*Mens rea* – recklessness

Pagett	Used girlfriend as shield	Causation – intervening act
Sweet v Parsley	Did not know students were taking drugs	Strict liability
Hill v Baxter	A swarm of bees	*Actus reus* – voluntary act
Roberts	Woman jumped from moving car	Causation – escape case
Miller	Set fire to his bed	*Actus reus* – omissions
Thabo Meli	Thought victim was dead so threw him over cliff	Coincidence of *actus reus* and *mens rea*
Hancock and Shankland	Taxi driver killed	*Mens rea* – oblique intent
Blaue	Refused blood transfusion	Causation – thin skull rule
Smith	Original wound was still operating and substantial	Causation – legal causation

2   Add some detail to the basic definitions shown below. (To achieve high marks you will need more than just a simple definition of the *actus reus* and *mens rea* of the relevant offence.)

Assault	
	Actus reus is any act which makes the victim apprehend the immediate infliction of unlawful force.
Two pieces of detail:	In *Logdon* a man showed his victim a gun in a drawer. The victim did not realise that this was a replica and became terrified.
	Words alone could be enough and even a silent phone call (*Ireland*).
	Mens rea is an intention to cause the victim to apprehend immediate, unlawful violence or recklessness as to whether such apprehension is caused.
Definition of intention:	Acting deliberately or making something your aim or purpose (*Mohan*).
Definition of recklessness:	Knowing there is a risk of the unlawful consequence, but continuing with the act (*Cunningham*).

Battery	
	Actus reus is the application of unlawful force.
Two pieces of detail:	A mere touch can be sufficient, e.g. tickling, kissing or throwing water over someone (*Collins v Willcocks*).
	It can be indirect (*Fagan/Thomas/DPP v K/Haystead*).
	Mens rea is intention or recklessness as to applying unlawful force.
Definition of intention:	Acting deliberately or making someone your aim or purpose (*Mohan*).

Battery	
Definition of recklessness:	Definition of recklessness: Knowing there is a risk of the unlawful consequence, but continuing with the act *(Cunningham)*.
Confirmed in:	*Venna*

Actual bodily harm s. 47	
	Actus reus is either assault or battery plus actual bodily harm.
Two pieces of detail:	Actual bodily harm includes 'any hurt or injury calculated to interfere with health or comfort. 'It has to be more than transient or trifling' *(Miller)*. Can include psychiatric injury *(Chan Fook)*.
	Mens rea – only the *mens rea* for assault or battery is needed.
Facts and conclusion in *Roberts*:	Facts and conclusion in *Roberts*: A man gave a girl a lift in his car and made sexual advances, touching her clothes. She feared rape and jumped from car and was injured. He argued that he saw no risk of injury, but court said that it was sufficient that he had the *mens rea* for battery.
Facts and conclusion in *Savage*.	Facts and conclusion in *Savage*: The defendant threw beer into the victim's face, which was battery, for which she had the *mens rea*. But she also let go of the glass and caused a cut to the victim's wrist and was convicted of ABH and again the court said that it was sufficient that she had the *mens rea* for the battery

Grievous bodily harm and wounding s. 20	
	Actus reus is either inflicting GBH or wounding.
Meaning of GBH:	GBH means serious harm *(Saunders)* and includes things like broken limbs, dislocations, permanent disability or scarring, substantial loss of blood.
Meaning of wounding:	Wounding means breaking the skin, not internal bleeding *(Eisenhower)*.
	Mens rea is intention or recklessness as to whether some harm caused.
Definition of intention:	Acting deliberately or making something your aim or purpose *(Mohan)*.
Definition of recklessness:	Knowing there is a risk of the unlawful consequence, but continuing with the act *(Cunningham)*.
Statement in *Mowatt*:	The defendant merely has to foresee some physical harm, albeit of a minor character.

Grievous bodily harm and wounding s. 18	
	Actus reus is either inflicting GBH or wounding.
Meaning of GBH:	GBH means serious harm *(Saunders)* and includes things like broken limbs, dislocations, permanent disability or scarring, substantial loss of blood.
Meaning of wounding:	Wounding means breaking the skin, not internal bleeding *(Eisenhower)*.
	Mens rea is either intention to cause GBH or intention to resist arrest.
Definition of intention:	Acting deliberately or making something your aim or purpose *(Mohan)*.
Definition of oblique intent:	The defendant claims to have some other purpose, but the jury are satisfied that the defendant knew serious injury was virtually certain *(Nedrick/Woollin)*.

10: The courts: procedure and sentencing

Now test yourself 1

1 Summary; either way; indictable

2 Bail Act 1976

3 There is a general right to bail.

4 If the defendant might abscond and not attend their trial; commit a further offence if granted bail, interfere with/threaten witnesses.

5 Surrender of passport; regular reporting to a police station

6 Yes, providing the magistrates feel that they have jurisdiction.

7 Crime and Disorder Act 1998.

8 Beyond reasonable doubt.

Now test yourself 2

1 Retribution; deterrence; rehabilitation

2 When the sentence is not activated unless the defendant commits further offences.

3 Three of the following: Community punishment orders, Community rehabilitation orders, Curfew requirements and Alcohol/drug treatment.

4 Absolute and Conditional

5 Any three of the following: first offence; defendant is very young or old; defendant has expressed remorse and made efforts to compensate the victim.

6 Any three of the following: offence involving an abuse of trust; use of a weapon; repeated attacks.

Check your understanding

1 In the table write three points about the criminal procedure for each of the types of offence.

Summary offences	
Point 1	Defendant may be represented for the first hearing by the duty solicitor at the court.
Point 2	If a guilty plea is made sentencing may take place immediately on first appearance or the magistrates may adjourn for pre-sentencing reports before they pass sentence.
Point 3	If a not guilty plea is entered the procedure may be adjourned for witnesses or for the defendant to obtain further legal advice. Magistrates will also decide whether the defendant should receive legal aid and be released on bail or kept in custody.

Either way offences	
Point 1	There is a plea before venue and the defendant is asked whether they plead guilty or not guilty. If a guilty plea is entered the defendant may be sentenced or sent to the Crown Court if the magistrates do not have sufficient powers.
Point 2	If a not guilty plea is entered the magistrates will carry out a mode of trial hearing to decide if the case is to be heard at the Magistrates' or the Crown Court. If either the defendant elects for Crown Court trial, or the magistrates decide that they do not have jurisdiction, the case will be sent to Crown Court.
Point 3	If the defendant elects for trial before magistrates and magistrates have accepted jurisdiction, the case will be adjourned for trial.

Indictable offences	
Point 1	The magistrates transfer the case to the Crown Court for a plea and directions hearing under the Crime and Disorder Act 1998.
Point 2	If a guilty plea is entered the judge will pass sentence, after a possible adjournment for pre-sentence report.
Point 3	If the defendant pleads not guilty, the case is adjourned. A jury will decide on guilt/innocence and if the defendant is found guilty the judge will pass sentence.

2 Write simple definitions for the sentencing terms shown below.

Term	Definition
Retribution	Offenders should be punished and get their 'just deserts' and receive the sentence their degree of fault deserves.
Individual deterrence	A sentence designed to prevent the offender from reoffending.
General deterrence	A sentence designed to send a warning to other people to discourage them from committing the offence.
Rehabilitation	The reform of the offender, so that they will not want to commit further offences.
Tariff	The sentence appropriate for the 'average' example of the offence.
Aggravating	Factors which make the offence more serious.
Mitigating	Circumstances which allow the court to impose a lower sentence.
Custody	Imprisonment
Suspended sentence	The sentence is not activated unless the defendant commits further offences.
Conditional discharge	No sentence is given, but if the offender commits a further offence in the stated period, then they can be resentenced for the original offence.

11: Liability in negligence

Now test yourself 1

1 You must take reasonable care to avoid acts or omissions which foreseeably could injure your neighbour.

2 That the damage or harm was reasonably foreseeable; that there was proximity between the claimant and defendant; and that it is just, fair and reasonable to impose a duty of care.

3 To prevent a flood of cases.

4 *Blyth v Birmingham Waterworks*

5 That a doctor is not liable for negligence if he has acted in accordance with a practice accepted as proper by a responsible body of medical opinion. '

6 That a child defendant will be compared to a reasonable child of the same age as the defendant.

7 Probability of harm; magnitude (or seriousness) of potential harm; cost and practicality of preventing the risk; potential benefits of the risk.

8 Because the patient would have died from arsenic poisoning whatever the doctor had tried to do. His breach was not the factual cause of death.

9 That if the kind of damage is foreseeable, it does not matter that it happened in an unforeseeable way.

Check your understanding

1 In the table below, identify the case being referred to and which area of law it applies to.

Facts	Name of case	Area of law
He should have been made to wear goggles	*Paris v Stepney*	Beach – seriousness of harm
To close the factory would be disproportionate	*Latimer v AEC*	Breach – cost/practicality of avoiding risk
Injured by cricket ball	*Bolton v Stone*	Breach – likelihood of harm
Injured chasing stolen car	*Langley v Dray*	Duty – foreseeability
He would have died anyway	*Barnett v Chelsea Hospital*	Damage – causation
A learner driver	*Nettleship v Weston*	Breach – reasonable person
Not sufficient warning for the blind	*Haley v London Electricity*	Breach – likelihood of harm
It was not foreseeable that it would ignite	*Wagon Mound*	Damage – remoteness
She was not in the immediate vicinity	*Bourhill v Young*	Duty – proximity
Decomposed snail	*Donoghue v Stevenson*	Duty – neighbour test
Burn caused cancer	*Smith v Leech Brain*	Damage – thin skull rule
Introduced three-part test	*Caparo v Dickman*	Duty

2 Use the word bank to fill in the missing words in this paragraph about the meaning of the term breach of duty.

Once duty of care has been proved, we must then prove that the defendant has breached their duty. To do this, we compare the defendant to the REASONABLE person. If they have not acted as an ordinary PRUDENT person would have done, they have breached their duty. In *Nettleship v Weston*, a LEARNER driver breached his duty because his driving was worse than an ordinary driver's; it was irrelevant that he was a learner.

If the defendant is a PROFESSIONAL person and has special SKILLS in his/her job, he/she is compared to a COMPETENT person in that profession (Bolam principle).

There are four RISK factors which can be used to make this comparison.

If there is a high degree of PROBABILITY that harm or damage will result (if harm is likely), the reasonable person would take extra care. In *Bolton v Stone*, cricket balls only escaped from the cricket ground six times in THIRTY years, so no extra care needed to be taken.

If any harm is likely to occur and be serious (the MAGNITUDE of likely harm), more precautions should be taken. Any harm to the one-eyed welder's eye would obviously be serious, so PROTECTION should have been offered.

Cost is balanced against PRACTICALITY. If the risk is cheap and easy to prevent, the reasonable person would prevent it. In *Latimer v AEC Ltd*, it was impractical and too EXPENSIVE to expect the factory to close when oil and water flooded the floor.

Sometimes risks are justified for the potential BENEFITS they bring, such as saving life or limb. In *Watt v Hertfordshire CC*, taking specialist equipment on a fire engine not suitable for it was a risk worth taking if they could get to an accident scene more quickly and SAVE a life.

12: The courts: procedure and damages

Now test yourself 1

1 Damages which can be precisely calculated from the tort up to trial; includes loss of earnings and medical costs.

2 Multiplying the average annual earnings lost (multiplicand) and the number of years of loss (multiplier).

3 The injury itself, pain and suffering and loss of amenity.

4 That the claimant takes reasonable steps to reduce his/her losses.

5 It would be a fast track action in the County Court.

6 This would be heard in the small claims track in the County Court.

7 *Dunnett v Railtrack*

8 Negotiation; mediation; conciliation

9 *Scott v London and St Katherine's Docks Co.*

10 The burden is placed on the defendant to demonstrate that there is another plausible explanation for the accident.

11 On the balance of probabilities.

Check your understanding

1 Complete the tables below.

Special damages	
What they are	Quantifiable losses up to date of trial
What they cover	Any costs/losses including medical costs and loss of earnings

General damages	
What they are	Future losses which cannot be precisely calculated
Pecuniary	Future financial losses including loss of earnings calculated using multiplicand and multiplier
Non-pecuniary	Future non-financial losses e.g. loss of amenity, pain and suffering

13: Formation of contract

Now test yourself 1

1 A contract between two parties where one party makes an offer and another party accepts.

2 A unilateral contract is where one party makes an offer but acceptance is through the performance of an act.

3 If it is firm, capable of being accepted and clear it requires certain conditions to be fulfilled. *Carlill v Carbolic Smoke Ball Co.* confirms this.

4 The person who accepts it must know about it.

5 An offer can be terminated by acceptance; refusal; counter offer; revocation; lapse of time.

6 An invitation to treat is an invitation to someone to make an offer

7 *Pharmaceutical Society v Boots*

8 If conditions are attached an acceptance becomes a counter offer.

9 The court decided that silence could not be acceptance.

10 Revocation means withdrawing the offer.

11 When instantaneous methods are used, acceptance is immediate as long as it is communicated.

12 A contract is made when the last of the forms is sent and received without objection.

Now test yourself 2

1 If it is made under deed.

2 As long as the consideration has some value, it is adequate. It does not need to be the market value.

3 Past consideration is something that has already been done before the agreement was entered into.

4 Because in *Hartley v Ponsonby* the sailors were expected to do something over and above their existing duties, whereas in *Stylk v Myrick* they were only carrying out their normal duties.

5 It allows them to enforce agreements where they are expressly identified as beneficiaries.

6 Agreements within families – domestic arrangements – are treated as not intending to create legal relations.

7 *Balfour* was a mere domestic arrangement. In *Merrit* the parties had separated and also by putting it in writing they indicated that they wanted it to be binding.

8 Details of expenses were agreed and confirmation of the agreement was put in writing.

9 The written agreement contained a clause that it was not entered into as a formal or legal agreement.

10 Football pools

Check your understanding

1 Complete the tables below.

Consideration rules	Case example	Facts of case that demonstrate rule
Must have value, but doesn't have to be adequate	*Chappell and Co. Ltd v Nestlé Co. Ltd*	Three chocolate bar wrappers were good consideration
It must not be past	*Re McArdle*	Agreement was not enforceable because the repairs to property had been done before the agreement was made
It must not be an existing duty	*Stilk v Myrick*	Sailors were already bound by their contract to sail back and to meet emergencies of the voyage. Promising to sail back after two of the crew deserted was not valid consideration

Elements of formation of contract	Definition
Offer	Expression of a willingness to enter into a legally binding agreement
Invitation to treat	An invitation to someone to make an offer
Acceptance	Unconditional and unqualified agreement to all the terms in the offer
Consideration	The idea that each party to a contract must contribute something of value to it

2 Match the cases with the facts and state the relevant area of law.

Case	Facts	Rule of law illustrated
Chappell v Nestlé	Three chocolate bar wrappers	Consideration
Household Fire Insurance v Grant	Letter lost in post	Postal rule – acceptance valid when posted
Felthouse v Bindley	If I don't hear ... the horse will be mine	Acceptance – cannot be by silence
Merritt v Merritt	Husband left wife and agreed to pay her income	Mere social arrangement – no intention to create legal relations
Re McArdle	Promise to help pay for improvements to house before agreement was made	Past consideration
Pharmaceutical Society v Boots	Drugs on shelves in a chemist	Invitation to treat
Entores v Miles Far East	Acceptance by telex	Acceptance by instantaneous method – valid when received
Fisher v Bell	Flick knives in shop window	Invitation to treat
Partridge v Crittenden	Advert to sell wild birds	Offer
McGowan v Buxton	Won model car	Commercial agreement intending to create legal relations
Byrne v van Tienhoven	Letter revoking offer received after acceptance	Postal rule – revocation valid when received; acceptance valid when posted
Carlill v Carbolic Smoke Ball Co.	Claimed reward of £100	Offer can be made to whole world. Acceptance can be by conduct
Hyde v Wrench	W offered to sell farm for £1000. H said £950	Counter offer

14: Breach of contract and the courts: procedure and damages

Now test yourself 1

1 When one party shows at some time before performance is due that he or she does not intend to observe his or her obligations under the contract.

2 To sue immediately he or she becomes aware that performance will not be carried out or to wait until the date for performance becomes due.

3 The right to repudiate the contract.

4 So far as money can do it, to place the claimant in the same situation with respect to damages as if the contract had been performed.

5 Damages should be awarded only for losses that could fairly and reasonably be considered to have arisen naturally or been in the contemplation of the parties at the time they made the contract.

6 *Hadley v Baxendale*

7 Losses that the supplier was not aware of, namely those relating to the dyeing contract.

8 Claimants must do all they reasonable can to minimise their losses.

9 The turbines that the claimants bought were more efficient than those that would have been supplied under the contract and saved them money.

10 That you are only expected to take reasonable steps to mitigate losses.

Now test yourself 2

1 Admit the claim and pay the money; defend the claim and serve a defence; do nothing, default is pay full amount.

2 Small claims; fast track; multi-track.

3 Small claims up to £10,000; fast track £10,000– £25,000; multi-track over £25,000

4 Multi-track

5 Negotiation; mediation; conciliation

6 On the balance of probabilities.

Check your understanding

1 Match the cases with the facts and areas of law

Case	Facts	Area of law
Hochster v de la Tour	Man was hired as courier	Anticipatory breach – able to sue immediately rather than wait for date of performance
Westinghouse v Underground Electric Railways	Turbines did not match specifications	Mitigation of damage – losses reduced by using more efficient turbines
Stansbie v Troman	Decorator given keys of house but failed to lock it	Causation of damage – failure to lock was cause of property being stolen
Victoria Laundry v Newman Industries	New boiler needed for dyeing contract	Remoteness of damage – defendants did not know about this contract and therefore were not liable for loss of profits on it
Bettini v Gye	An opera singer missed the first two rehearsals	Breach of warranty – only a minor inconvenience, not going to root of contract
Poussard v Spiers and Pond	An opera singer whose role was central missed the first six performances	Breach of condition – singer's role was very important and therefore missing six performances went to root of contract

2 Complete the table to show how damages are calculated.

Stages	Explanation of rule	Case which confirms rule
1 The purpose of damages	Put claimant in the same situation as if the contract had been performed	*Robinson v Harman*
2 Causation	There must be a causal link between the breach of contract and the damage suffered	*Stansbie v Troman*
3 Remoteness	Losses are recoverable if they are reasonably within the contemplation of the parties as a probable result of the breach	*Hadley v Baxendale* *Victoria Laundry v Newman Industries*
4 Mitigation	Claimant has duty to do what is reasonable to ensure that as far as possible losses are kept to a minimum	*British Westinghouse v Underground Electric Railway of London* *Pilkington v Wood*